MW00636811

The Complete Writing Program

— The Workshop Approach —

by David S. Dye M.ED.

MODEL
CITIZEN
PUBLICATIONS

Dedication

This book is dedicated to and inspired by my wife, Joy, and my sons, Shawn and Ryan. My wife's infinite patience and my commitment to teach my students the way I would want my own children to be taught is what made this book a reality.

Table of Contents

Preface

My first year of teaching, I had to plan an effective writing program for my middle school students. I had no clue where to begin. As I prepared for those seventh grade students, I had to ask several important questions. What should they be able to do by now? What should they be able to do by the end of the year? How do I get them there? What resources are available to help me figure this out?

Just as I began to get a handle on the seventh grade, I was transferred to the fourth grade, and the entire process started again. To help prepare myself for what I should be teaching I begged, borrowed, and stole ideas from other teachers. I collected and created material. I scribbled lesson ideas on napkins at restaurants and on the back of church bulletins while the pastor preached (no doubt creating a false impression in his mind that I was a diligent note taker, absorbing every word of his sermon.) After eight years of trial and error, I finally had a writing program that I was proud to present.

Why was I proud of this program? It clearly worked. I finally had the tools I needed to measure the writing ability of my students in September, and apply the same measurement in June to rate the amount of progress they had made. I finally had a vehicle in which the students were required to apply writing and grammar skills into their writing. I must say that, as a teacher, it is so exciting to see my students apply skills on a daily basis when so many other students forget each skill as soon as the teacher stops focusing on it. Lastly, my excitement over this writing program grows stronger every year because I can see that my students are developing good writing habits that will last them the rest of their lives.

The hardest part of the program for me is the knowledge that I only have ten months with my students to put them on the path of great writing. This is a big reason why I have placed an emphasis in this program on home school parents. They are the ones who can see their students evolve and develop the most within this program. There is enough information in this book to last their children a lifetime. True, the worksheets may be finished in a year or two, but the beauty of this program is that any new writing skill discovered can simply be incorporated into the program as easily as adding another shelf to a closet. Consider this program the closet. The worksheets that follow are the start of your wardrobe. Through your creativity and the other resources you find, you will give your students such a depth of writing knowledge that their "closet" will become a garage.

It is my tremendous pleasure to offer this program to you. I sincerely pray that you will enjoy the success that I have had. Let's start building that closet...

Chapter 1
Writing Assessment

This chapter will:

    1. Explain the heart of this writing program - The Writing Assessment Checklist.

    2. Prepare you to teach your students how to improve in all genres of writing.

    3. Prepare students to critique their own writing intelligently as well as the writing of others.

    4. Begin developing good writing habits that will last a lifetime.

* This section will begin by explaining <u>how this writing program works</u> and will close with a sample lesson plan about <u>how to begin</u> teaching it to your students.

** The following chapters give you the tools you need to make all five parts of the Writing Assessment Checklist work for your students.

Introduction

When I was in the third grade, my teacher gave a writing assignment. I sat in my seat and worked as hard as I could to make it the greatest piece of writing a third grader could create. With my heart full of pride and a smile stretching from ear to ear, I made the trek to the teacher's desk, awaiting the praise I was sure would be given. She scanned my brown, fat-lined paper and with a dry, expressionless face said, "Make it better."

"Make it better? How can I make it better?" I wondered as I stumbled back to my seat. I did the best job I could on the first draft. For the next ten minutes I sat and studied my writing without a clue about how to "make it better."

I've played this scene in my head for many years while creating this writing program. I swore that I would never ask students to "make it better" without giving them the tools to do it. I would be specific as to what I wanted. I would be clear about how they should do it. Most of all, I would show my students specifically why their changes made their writing better.

As Ecclesiastes says, "There's nothing new under the sun." This can be said about my writing program. I've studied close to a hundred writing rubrics from school districts all over the country, and I've studied numerous other writing programs. While none of them accomplished specifically what I wanted, many of them contained great ideas.

When my writing program was finally in place, I realized that I had a program that was uniquely my own. The students knew exactly what it took to be a great writer. They were learning to recognize text that had the elements of great writing. They were going back to their first drafts and rewriting sentences, adding or deleting sentences, and changing vocabulary based on what they already knew about great writing.

Your students will do the same thing. Take your time getting comfortable with this chapter. Once you have a solid understanding of the <u>Writing Assessment Checklist</u>, the rest of the program will fall into place much more easily. Have fun.

Writing Assessment Checklist

1. Did the writer completely cover the topic?
2. Did the writer use Show-Not-Tell sentences?
3. How is the writer's vocabulary?
4. Did the writer use Writing Tricks?
5. Overall, how did the writer do?

The writing Assessment Chart

Name _____

Writing Assessment Sheet

Type of writing being assessed - _____

_____

Instructions:

Overview

Take a moment to review the three sheets above (also located on the next three pages). Tell your students, "These three papers will be your best friends this year." Go on to explain that these sheets will guide them to knowledge about writing that they never knew they could achieve. After a few more motivational words, proceed to explain the papers, one at a time.

Do this near the beginning of the school year. You will be able to identify your highly motivated students just by looking into their eyes. These are the students who are sitting up straight, eyes wide, ready to assess the writing in front of them. These are future teachers in the making who will be your outstanding assistants for the next several months.

First, explain the Writing Assessment Checklist. It explains the five things that great writers do. The second paper is the Writing Assessment Chart. It tells them what score to give each part of the Writing Assessment Checklist. The third paper is the Writing Assessment Sheet that keeps track of the scores and explains the reason for each.

Note: If you just study the three sheets for a few minutes, you can probably get the idea about how the program will work. The rest of the chapter gives a detailed explanation of the program, samples of student writing that have been assessed, and tricks of the trade.

These three sheets work together to give students a basic concept of good writing. Everything we do in class is designed to strengthen each aspect of the Writing Assessment Checklist. Consistent growth in these five areas of writing will prepare our elementary and middle school students for the challenges of high school, college, and beyond.

Writing Assessment Checklist

1. Did the writer completely cover the topic?

2. Did the writer use Show-Not-Tell sentences?

3. How is the writer's vocabulary?

4. Did the writer use Writing Tricks?

5. Overall, how did the writer do?

The Writing Assessment Chart

6 Spectacular

- *The writing went <u>way above and beyond</u> expectations.*
- The sentences paint a picture in the mind as if watching it happen in front of me.
- **Advanced Vocabulary**
- The writer used advanced "writing tricks". (i.e. Metaphors, Compound Sentences, Introductory Phrases, etc.)

5 Skilled

- *The writing went <u>above and beyond</u> expectations.*
- Many show-not-tell sentences were used.
- **Strong Vocabulary**
- The writer used many "writing tricks". (i.e. Metaphors, Compound Sentences, Introductory Phrases, etc.)

4 Capable

- *The writing was organized and covered the topic.*
- The sentences were well written and described the topic clearly.
- **Good Vocabulary**
- The writer used a few "writing tricks". (i.e. Metaphors, Compound Sentences, Introductory Phrases, etc.).

3 Growing

- *The writer covered <u>most</u> of the topic.*
- The sentences were complete and understandable.
- **The vocabulary had some descriptive words.**
- All the sentences were very similar to each other.

2 Limited

- *The writing was <u>less</u> than expected.*
- Many simple sentences.
- **Simple Vocabulary**
- The ideas in the writing were simple.

1 Not Functional

- Almost nothing was written.
- Poor penmanship made the writing hard to read.
- It is difficult to understand what the writer is trying to say.

Name _____

Writing Assessment Sheet

Type of writing being assessed: _____

_____

Instructions:
1. Read through the writing once. Edit by checking for spelling and punctuation errors.
2. Check the writing for the five items below. Write the score that best describes the writing in the box to the right.
3. In the space on the right, explain why you gave the author the score listed in the box.

	Score	Explain the Score
1. The writer completely covered the topic.		
2. The sentences were well written and had show-not-tell.		
3. Vocabulary		
4. The writing had style including writing tricks.		
5. Overall Impressions (Include spelling, punctuation, and interest level.)		
Total Score		5) Total =

For the Author:
    On a separate sheet of paper, write a paragraph describing your writing. What were your strong points, and what parts of your writing need improvement?

Teaching Students How To Assess Writing

Outline

Before taking the time to learn each step of the program, it would be helpful to become comfortable with the steps involved. It may seem overwhelming as you read the detailed explanation of the program, but teaching students to assess each other's writing can be broken down into five steps. You will have the students:

1. **Memorize the Writing Assessment Checklist.**

   In this step, your students will become comfortable with the five elements of great writing.

2. **Learn to use the Writing Assessment Sheet.**

   Your students will learn to search for each element of great writing within their partners' writing.

3. **Learn to score each of the five elements of great writing using the Writing Assessment Chart.**

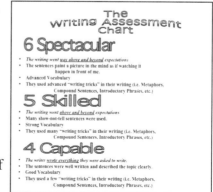

4. **Give the writing an over-all score.**

5. **Use the Writing Assessment Sheet as a guide to improve their own writing.**

   The students will use this worksheet to spot areas of their writing that need to be revised. Most of this book contains lessons that help build students' skills in the five areas of great writing. The students will use the lessons you've taught to help improve their writing.

How It Works:

Writing Assessment Checklist

1. Did the writer completely cover the topic?
2. Did the writer use Show-Not-Tell sentences?
3. How is the writer's vocabulary?
4. Did the writer use Writing Tricks?
5. Overall, how did the writer do?

Before you try to understand how this program works, read the five items on the Writing Assessment Checklist above …

… read it again …

… read it again …

… read it one more time …

The Writing Assessment Checklist is the heart of this writing program. It takes the guesswork out of deciding what makes a good piece of writing. Also, it specifically tells the students what they are doing well and what parts of their writing need work. Many of my older students like the fact that it takes much of the subjective bias out of grading their writing. Students will often challenge their scores which provides me with a great "teachable moment". I am able to give clear explanations to a student eager to learn.

It is crucial for you and your students to understand the Writing Assessment Checklist. I make my students memorize it as soon as possible. By the second day of presenting this program, many students are able to repeat it in five to ten seconds. (They enjoy racing my stopwatch, and many students who haven't memorized the checklist are eager to memorize it for the next time we race.) A thorough understanding of the Writing Assessment Checklist is the first step in developing great writing skills.

Let's go over each point on the Writing Assessment Checklist. I will explain the concepts related to each point. I repeat these concepts over and over again throughout the year until my students know them by heart. While reviewing these concepts, my students will often finish my sentences for me. This is what I want because I only have ten months to get them to master the five elements of great writing.

Read this section carefully and re-read it until you feel that you can explain it. When you are finished, see if you can repeat the five steps of the Writing Assessment Checklist and summarize what each step means. To keep these concepts fresh in the students' minds, give them little quizzes asking them about the concepts in this section.

You should begin this writing program by giving each student a copy of the Writing Assessment Checklist (Page 6) and spending about fifteen minutes going over it. Below are some of the points I try to make, which I review on a regular basis. Also, the way I'm presenting this to you here is the way I present it to my students. You can use this as your lesson plan or use the sample lesson plan at the end of this chapter.

1. Did the writer completely cover the topic?

completely cover the topic

A. An important part of writing is <u>knowing your audience and what they expect from you</u>. Is it an essay for a teacher? A letter to a friend? A poem written for your own satisfaction? Or a district-wide writing test to assess your writing abilities? You must be able to cover the topic to the satisfaction of your audience. Students will get a 4 on the assessment sheet if they do a good job, a 5 if they cover the expectations very well, or a 3 if they fall a little short.

B. <u>What should a student be able to do by his/her age or grade?</u> Meeting grade level expectations is an important part of completely covering the topic. A third grader should be able to write a good, well-organized paragraph. For him, this would be a 4 on the assessment sheet. A fourth grader should be able to write three complete paragraphs in a forty-five minute timed essay. For her, anything less would be a 3 or a 2.

 By now, the students are beginning to see that the amount they write and the accuracy of their writing does affect the quality of their writing and keeps them accountable when they are scored.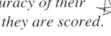

Now look at the Writing Assessment Chart. This is where they look to find the score that the writer deserves. When you score your students' writing AND when the students score each other's writing, this is what is used to give the score.

What do you notice about the FIRST bullet under each number? The first bullet comments on how well the writer covered the topic. Always, always, always, look at the 4 first, which means "Capable." If the comment about the 4 applies, then you can read the 5 "Skilled" or the 6 "Spectacular" to see if either apply. If the comment about the 4 does not apply, then read the comments under the 3 or the 2 to see if they apply.

Note: A 6 is meant for those students who reach top form and should be used sparingly. Also, the 1 basically means that the student wrote almost nothing.

> ### The Writing Assessment Chart
> **6 Spectacular**
> * The writing was way above and beyond expectations.
> **5 Skilled**
> * The writing went above and beyond expectations.
> **4 Capable**
> * The writing was organized and covered the topic.
> **3 Growing**
> * The writing covered most of the topic.
> **2 Limited**
> * The writing was less than expected.
> **1 Not Functional**
> * Almost nothing was written.

2. Did the writer use Show-Not-Tell sentences?

This section is titled "Show-Not-Tell Sentences", but it actually refers to the quality of the writers' sentences. The students should be extremely aware that we paint pictures with our words. These are the things that should be taken into consideration when assessing this part of the students' writing. *Note: Remind students that they are only examining the quality of sentences. If the scorer gave someone a 5 or a 3 for "Cover the Topic", the writer will now earn a score based ONLY on the quality of his/her sentences.*

A. The quality of their sentences should be appropriate to the age of the students. A fifth grader who writes only short, simple sentences would earn a low score. A sixth grader who mixes in a variety of sentence structures, including compound and complex sentences, would receive a higher score.

B. Did the writer paint a picture? Did the writer show what was happening rather than just tell?

For example: A student might write, "I was sad." He is telling how he felt. The writer can show how he felt without saying, "I was sad." He could write, "My bottom lip began to quiver. Tears began to well up in my eyes. Barely able to breathe, I knelt down to see if my dog was okay." (There is a list of ideas about how to teach this later in the book.)

C. The sentences should show some understanding of the topic. My less motivated fifth graders amaze me with the number of different ways they can say the same thing. For example, they might write a paragraph that says: "I was bored. I had nothing to do. When I tried to think of something to do, I couldn't. I was so bored. I wished I had something to do." Knowing they had to turn in five sentences, they felt that they had completed the assignment. When they receive a "2" for sentences, and are told that they cannot go to recess until they make it a "4", they decide that they can become a little more creative with the quality of their sentences. The sentences should show a well-rounded knowledge of the topic.

After reading the piece a SECOND time, only focusing on the quality of their sentences, the students will look at the Writing Assessment Chart to find the score that the author deserves. What do you notice about the second bullet under each number? The second bullet under each number refers to the quality of the student's sentence. Remember, always look at the 4 because this means that the writer did a good job. If we can say yes to the 4, then we can read the 5 or the 6 to see which applies to this piece of writing. If we cannot say yes to the 4, then we determine if the 3 or the 2 applies.

[handwritten margin notes: "paint a picture", "Understanding of the topic"]

The
Writing Assessment
Chart

6 Spectacular
* The writing was way above and beyond expectations.
* The sentences paint a picture in the mind...

5 Skilled
* The writing went above and beyond expectations.
* Many show-not-tell sentences were used.

4 Capable
* The writing was organized and covered the topic.
* The sentences were well written...

3 Growing
* The writing covered most of the topic.
* The sentences were complete and understandable.

2 Limited
* The writing was less than expected.
* Many simple sentences.

1 Not Functional
* Almost nothing was written.
* The writing was hard to read.

3. How is the writer's vocabulary?

Having a well developed vocabulary helps with effective communication, shows intelligence, and provides a variety of ways to make your point. This is the area of student writing that tends to need the most help. When students realize that their writing score improves when they use strong vocabulary words, they become more motivated to apply classroom vocabulary words learned throughout the year, and the thesaurus becomes a more valuable resource.

Here are some ideas to share with your students about how to assess this section:

A. If the average student two years below your grade level can understand <u>every word</u> in your writing, it probably does not have well developed vocabulary. (I've found this comment really builds a fire under some students, especially the ones who have younger brothers or sisters.)

B. There is a <u>difference between <u>descriptive</u> vocabulary and <u>strong</u> vocabulary. For example, the word "slimy" is descriptive, but the average third-grader could tell you what it means. "Sludgy" or "repulsive" might be a stronger vocabulary word. *Note: Sometimes the descriptive word, while more simple, is the best choice. The art of writing is knowing when to use a simple word and when to be more sophisticated.*

difference between descriptive & strong vocab

Every pair of students in my class shares a thesaurus, which is placed between them on their desk. This is a good time to explain that the thesaurus is an excellent resource for finding better vocabulary words.

thesaurus

By now, the pattern for assessing the writing should be obvious. The person assessing the writing will read the writing a THIRD time, ONLY looking for the quality of vocabulary words. This part is simple to score if students circle three or four of the author's best vocabulary words. If all are easily understood, they have an idea about how to score this section. Following the same pattern, the third bullet under each number relates to the quality of the vocabulary within the writing.

The Writing Assessment Chart

6 Spectacular
* The writing was way above and beyond expectations.
* The sentences paint a picture in the mind...
* Advanced Vocabulary

5 Skilled
* The writing went above and beyond expectations.
* Many show-not-tell sentences were used.
* Strong Vocabulary

4 Capable
* The writing was organized and covered the topic.
* The sentences were well written...
* Good Vocabulary

3 Growing
* The writing covered most of the topic.
* The sentences were complete and understandable.
* The vocabulary had some descriptive words.

2 Limited
* The writing was less than expected.
* Many simple sentences.
* Simple Vocabulary

1 Not Functional
* Almost nothing was written.
* The writing was hard to read.
* You can't figure out what the writer is trying to say.

---

4. Did the writer use Writing Tricks?

This is my favorite part of the assessment because it's an area where the students begin to see immediate results. A "writing trick" is just any intelligently written sentence. When a writer does something clever to get her point across, it's a writing trick. The use of <u>dialogue</u> is a writing trick. So is using <u>similes</u> and <u>metaphors</u>. Strategically placed <u>adjectives</u> or <u>exciting verbs</u> can also be writing tricks. Any writing skill can be made into a writing trick. An entire chapter is devoted to writing tricks later in the book. Now might be a good time to review that section just to become more familiar with writing tricks.

Below is an example of a paragraph that contains writing tricks. When I teach the students a new writing trick, I require that they use it at least two times in their next few writing assignments. They must underline it and write the trick's name below. Here is an example of a homework assignment which called for the student to write a paragraph about an exciting moment while camping. The student was to use the writing tricks Dialogue, Simile/Metaphor, and Adjectives.

<u>"There's a snake in my bed!"</u> screamed Sarah as she began pounding furiously on
(Attention Getter and Dialogue)
her sleeping bag. My heart pounding, I raced into her tent <u>like a bolt of lighting</u>. There was
(Simile/Metaphor)
hissing coming from somewhere, so I grabbed Sarah's <u>skinny, trembling arm</u> and pulled her
(Adjectives)
outside the tent. By now Mom, Dad, and my two brothers surrounded the space where the

serpent lurked, each carrying a weapon to pound its evil head. <u>"On the count of three, be ready to</u>
(Dialogue)
<u>strike!"</u> yelled my father <u>like a general going to war.</u> On "three" the sleeping bag came up, and
(Simile/Metaphor)
we all pounded that snake with all our might. When the dust settled, we were all embarrassed to

find that we had just killed my sister's <u>leaky air mattress</u>.
(Adjectives)

This section is difficult for the students to score at the beginning of the year because they have not learned many tricks yet. However, by the third month I've taught about five or six tricks, and they begin to get the idea. While they may struggle at first deciding what is and what is not a writing trick, the teacher understands that any part of the writing that gives the piece some personality is considered a writing trick. Also, the more comfortable the students become with the program, the better they will be about explaining and detecting writing tricks.

How should the students score this part of the writing assessment? I tell them to read the remarks next to the forth bullet under each number, and give it their best guess. I assure them it's not brain surgery, and that the score they give will not be registered on the partners' report cards. In a few weeks they will become more comfortable with the assessment process, and their worries will be over.

If you look at the Writing Assessment Chart, you will notice that the fourth bullet refers to the style of the writing. If the students used a variety of sentences (writing tricks), they will receive a score of 4 or better. If the sentences do not show much creativity, their score will drop accordingly.

5. Overall, how did the writer do? *How well it was written.*

This last section gives the students the chance to help edit the writing, make judgments about how well it was written, and determine how much they liked the piece. These are some things I encourage them to consider:

(1) A. Spelling and Punctuation. For first drafts, such as timed essays, I remind the students that a few errors are to be expected. However, the age of the student should be considered when determining how much is too much. Then again, a flawless first draft would warrant consideration of a higher score.

(2) B. How much did you enjoy this writing? Maybe the author has been getting 3's and 4's, but the reader enjoyed the story tremendously. Here, the reader can give the writing a 5 or 6. However, maybe the author has been getting 5's and 6's, but the writing was very dry and boring. This is where a 2 or 3 may be appropriate.

By now, the students should realize that a 4 indicates the author did a good job. Therefore, the score they should first consider giving for overall quality is 4. Encourage them to base their decision on the bullets which describe the criteria for each score on the Writing Assessment Chart. They can also rely on the titles (i.e. Capable, Skilled, Limited) to guide them.

The Accident
by Jane Doe

My friend named Rebecca and I were playing. In our apartments there are hard, rough, red bricks. We were rollerblading. My friend got on the bricks. I knew she was going to get hurt. I said get down. She just didn't want to go. I was feeling so solemn.

She laughed like a hyena. She said, "no, I won't get hurt!" I thought that she was going to fall on the cement and break some bones. So I got on too so if she was going to fall I would catch her. I was so scared so I fell off. She said, " can jump off too." I went to get her mom because she was on skates.

She said no and jumped off. She laughed at first and them cried. She screamed so loud that you could hear her from Maine. Her mother came and picked her up. She went to the hospital and got a cast. I felt so guilty about it. Everybody blamed it on me.

Let's Score One Together

What should a completed assessment sheet look like? On the over-head projector, assess an essay with the students to model the assessment process. Also, it gives you a chance to review what you just covered in a more practical setting.

Here is an example of how to score a fifth-grader's essay. The essay to the left was written about three months into the school year. After we assess her essay, she will know exactly what she did well and exactly where she needs to improve. Begin by making sure everyone has a copy of the essay (See Appendix), Writing Assessment Chart, Writing Assessment Checklist, and Assessment Sheet.

First, we read #1 on the Writing Assessment Checklist together. "Did the writer **completely cover** the topic?" Review with them what fifth graders should know about essays. In 45 minutes, they should be able to write three well organized paragraphs, and they should have included all the information required in the essay.

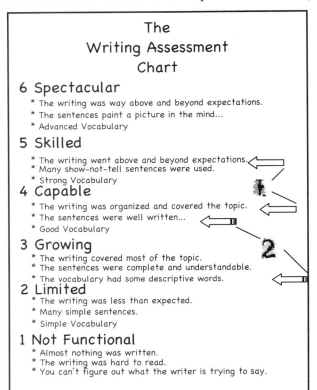

The
Writing Assessment
Chart

6 Spectacular
* The writing was way above and beyond expectations.
* The sentences paint a picture in the mind...
* Advanced Vocabulary

5 Skilled
* The writing went above and beyond expectations.
* Many show-not-tell sentences were used.
* Strong Vocabulary

4 Capable
* The writing was organized and covered the topic.
* The sentences were well written...
* Good Vocabulary

3 Growing
* The writing covered most of the topic.
* The sentences were complete and understandable.
* The vocabulary had some descriptive words.

2 Limited
* The writing was less than expected.
* Many simple sentences.
* Simple Vocabulary

1 Not Functional
* Almost nothing was written.
* The writing was hard to read.
* You can't figure out what the writer is trying to say.

Have them read the essay and determine if the author did a good job. The student was asked to write an essay describing a time she tried to help someone. She was to describe the problem, the steps she took to help, and how the situation ended. Are all three items included in this essay? Are all of the paragraphs well written?

In this case, three complete paragraphs were written and all of the information required was included. Ask the students, "What number do we read first?" We read bullet #1 under 4 "Capable" first. It says, "The writing was organized and covered the topic." We can say "yes" to this, so we move up to 5 "Skilled" which says, "The writing went above and beyond expectations." Because the writer wrote the minimum of what she was asked to write, I would not say "yes" to this statement. Therefore, the score would remain a 4. We would then put a 4 in the first box, and write an explanation on the right

describing why she received that score. Note: Some students will argue whether or not it's a 5 "Skilled." They think the writing is "... above and beyond" because it was a good story. This disagreement is fine

	Score	Explain the Score
1. The writer completely covered the topic.	4	She covered the topic. Three complete paragraphs and the topic has been covered.

because now they are making judgments about writing. They will soon be applying those same judgments to their own writing. I encourage students to challenge the scores because the more they challenge the Assessment Chart, the better they will become at assessing. It also gives you a chance to clarify any misunderstandings.

On their Assessment Sheet, allow them to enter either the 4 or the 5. Remember, it's not brain surgery, and your score as the teacher is the only one that counts for their report card.

Now have the students read #2 on the Writing Assessment Checklist together. It says, "Did the writer use **show-not-tell sentences**?" Have them read the sentences and determine if most of the sentences are short and simple or if some are well written. Also, do the sentences paint a picture? Have the students underline three or four of the best sentences and use them to determine the score. Have them read the second bullet under #4 "Capable", and determine if that description fits.

In this student's case, the sentences are average and there are some descriptive phrases.

A 4 "Capable" might be a fair score, but there were several short, simple sentences. Just to be sure, I would have the students read 3 "Growing." It says that the sentences are complete and understandable which, I feel, describes the sentences better. Also, I know that the writer is going to receive credit for the several writing tricks later, so I feel better about giving the lower score on the quality of her sentences. Once again, keep in mind that if any student can argue why he/she thinks the score should be a 3 "Growing" or a 5 "Skilled," allow the student to write that score on the Assessment Sheet. Once the students have written their scores, have them explain to the class why the scores were given.

	Score	Explain the Score
1. The writer completely covered the topic.	4	He/She wrote everything he/she was asked to write: Three complete paragraphs and the topic has been covered.
2. The sentences were well written and had show-not-tell.	3	The sentences were complete and understandable. Some sentences were short and simple.

Now read #3 on the Writing Assessment Checklist together as a class. "How is the writer's **vocabulary**?" Quickly review how to assess this part, and remind them that they are ONLY grading the vocabulary. Have your students circle the best vocabulary words before scoring this section. Circling the best words will help remind them that they are assessing only vocabulary.

Some of the best words circled by my students were "solemn", "hyena", "guilty", "scared", and "blamed." Read the third bullet under #4 "Capable" together, and ask the students if it applies to this essay. My fifth grade students generally agree that these words may be descriptive, but on the whole, they can't be considered "good". The writer did use one of our vocabulary words for the week, solemn, but most of the words were not that

The Writing Assessment Chart

6 Spectacular
* The writing was way above and beyond expectations.
* The sentences paint a picture in the mind...
* Advanced Vocabulary
* The writer used advanced writing tricks in the writing.

5 Skilled
* The writing went above and beyond expectations.
* Many show-not-tell sentences were used.
* Strong Vocabulary
* The writer used many writing tricks in the writing.

4 Capable
* The writer wrote everything he/she was asked to write.
* The sentences were well written...
* Good Vocabulary
* The writer used a few writing tricks in the writing.

3 Growing
* The writing described almost everything he/she was asked to write.
* The sentences were complete and understandable.
* The vocabulary had some descriptive words.
* All the sentences were very similar to each other.

2 Limited
* The writing was less than expected.
* Many simple sentences.
* Simple Vocabulary
* The ideas in the writing were simple.

1 Not Functional
* Almost nothing was written.
* The writing was hard to read.
* You can't figure out what the writer is trying to say.

sophisticated for a fifth grader. Therefore, we drop down to #3 "Growing" which states: "The vocabulary had some descriptive words." This seems to apply. However, encourage the students to read the third bullet under #2 "Limited" to see if it applies. Some students may feel that "simple vocabulary" is more appropriate. For these students, allow

	Score	Explain the Score
1. The writer completely covered the topic.	4	He/She wrote everything he/she was asked to write: Three complete paragraphs and the topic has been covered.
2. The sentences were well written and had show-not-tell.	3	The sentences were complete and understandable. Some sentences were short and simple.
3. Vocabulary	3	Some descriptive words. "Solemn, screamed, blamed"

them to enter a "2" on the Assessment Sheet.

When the students write their proofs to explain why they gave a certain score for vocabulary, simply have them write the three best words from the essay. This provides the best justification for their scoring.

Next, read #4 (**writing tricks**) on the Writing Assessment Checklist together as a class, review how to assess this part of the student writing, and encourage them to give their best guess. Remind them to look at the fourth bullet under all the numbers beginning with 4 "Capable", moving up or down the Assessment Chart accordingly.

Now would be a good time to make a list on the board of "writing tricks" the students already know (even though they may not think of them as writing tricks.) Many of my fifth graders at the beginning of the year are familiar with how to write dialogue, adjectives, similes, and other "tricks." If they can't find any of these in the writing, then I ask them to just consider the style of the writing. Does it have personality? Are there sentences in the writing that they find clever? Does the author get the point across in an interesting way?

3. Vocabulary	3	Some descriptive words. "Solemn, screamed, blamed
4. The writing had style, including writing tricks.	4	A few writing tricks were used. Simile, Dialogue, Hyperbole

After giving the students a few minutes to make their assessments, ask for volunteers to share their opinions with the class. There are a few writing tricks in this essay so anything lower than 3 "Growing" would be a harsh score to give a fifth grader. On the other hand, this piece is not so sophisticated that it should receive a 5 "Skilled". A 4 "Capable" would be a fair score for this sample.

After putting the score on the assessment sheet, be sure to have them write a sentence that explains why they gave their score. A list of the writing tricks that were used would also be appropriate rather than the sentence.

This is a good opportunity for you to help calibrate their scoring ability. It is also a good idea to point out some sentences that are examples of writing tricks.

The last item to assess is "**Overall**, how did the writer do?" Read #5 on the Writing Assessment Chart together and have them make a judgment about the overall quality of this writing sample. By reminding them that someone will be doing the same thing to their future writing, they will take this exercise very seriously and are much more honest about the assessment process. Below is a brief explanation of how I have them assess this part of the writing.

When my students assess each other's writing, I have them use a highlighter to mark spelling and punctuation. If there are many grammatical errors, I encourage the students to be strict about the scoring. In a first draft, a few mistakes are to be expected. However, if it is painfully obvious that the writer is struggling with grammar, the assessment needs to reflect this shortcoming with a lower score.

4. The writing had style, including writing tricks.	4	A few writing tricks were used. Simile, Dialogue, Hyperbole
5. Overall impressions. (Include spelling, punctuation, and interest level.	4	Good spelling and I liked the story very much.

In the sample essay, there are a few mistakes but nothing too drastic. Therefore, we can consider the following questions: 1. Did she leave out any information that was important to the story? 2. Was there anything in the story that you would have liked to have known more about? 3. Did you enjoy the story? 4. Did the story keep your attention? 5. Is there anything you noticed about the writing that you would like the author to know?

In the case of our sample, ask the students to comment about the essay. Go over these questions in the paragraph above and come up with a group decision. Again, if any students want to break with the group and assign their own score, encourage them to do so. I only ask that they explain why they are giving a different score. Most of my classes agree that this essay is a good story. Most people can identify with the author because she was blamed for something that was not her fault. I remind them that a "skilled" writer could have gone into a little more detail in certain areas. For example, what injury did Rebecca receive when she fell? Who is "everybody", and what did "they" say when they blamed her? Overall, the writer showed she was "Capable"; Therefore, I gave it a 4.

Scoring

Determining the final score on the Assessment Sheet requires a little math. I have a poster (see the appendix for the Conversion Chart) that I display because the division is a little tricky for elementary school students. The students who need it have a copy in their writing folders. All they need to do is add the numbers, and the poster provides the score. My middle school and high school students are expected to manage this without the poster.

Step 1 - Add the 5 numbers and put the score in the box marked "Total". In our sample, the five numbers are: 4, 3, 3, 4, 4 for a total of 18. *(Note: Some students may have different scores.)*

Step 2 - Divide the total by 5. In this case:

$$18 \div 5 = 3.6$$

Note: Many elementary school students will need a poster to help them figure out step 3.

Step 3 - Round the number to the nearest whole number. In this case 3.6 is closer to a 4. Because the score is below a 4, we call this piece of writing a **4-**.

	Score	Explain the Score
1. The writer completely covered the topic.	4	He/She wrote everything he/she was asked to write: Three complete paragraphs and the topic has been covered.
2. The sentences were well written and had show-not-tell.	3	The sentences were complete and understandable. Some sentences were short and simple.
3. Vocabulary	3	Some descriptive words. "Solemn, screamed, blamed"
4. The writing had style, including writing tricks.	4	He/She used a few writing tricks. Simile, Dialogue, Hyperbole
5. Overall impressions. (Include spelling, punctuation, and interest level.	4	Good spelling and punctuation. liked the story very much.
Total Score	18	5 ⟌ 18

One Step Beyond

Now is a great time to show the students how improving in one area affects the entire score. For example, if Jane Doe had written sentences that were more descriptive, the second score would have been a 4 instead of a 3. Writing more descriptions about the setting and the events would improve her score to a 5. By re-working the assessment sheet, the score is now a 20. $20 \div 5 = 4$. She has improved her score from a 4- to a 4.

Now you can demonstrate on the chalkboard how improving each part of their writing by one point will affect their overall score.

Old Score			New Score		
4			5		
3	Total		4	Total	
3	$18 \div 5 = 3.6$		4	$23 \div 5 = 4.6$	
4	**4-**		5	**5-**	
4			5		

Improving by one full score is a major achievement. This is the speech I now give to my students. Feel free to borrow any part of it.

"Becoming a great writer takes time and practice. To improve by one point on the assessment scale takes a great deal of work, but now you know how to do it. You now know how to make your writing better. All the guesswork is gone. Those of you who are serious about becoming great writers now know exactly what you must do to achieve your goal. If you work at writing everything you are supposed to write; compose quality sentences that paint pictures; improve your vocabulary; and use writing tricks such as dialogue and adjectives, you WILL become a great writers."

After a dramatic pause, tell them that they will have a writing test at the end of the year when they will have one hour to write on a topic. Next month I will give them a writing goal. If they are at level 3 now, their goal will be a 4. If they are at a 4- now, then their goal will be a 5-. Everyone has the same opportunity to achieve his or her goal. How hard they work during the year will determine how they do on that test. Those students who reach their goal will be invited to a celebration and get to choose how we celebrate. (The students who don't accomplish the goal are given a writing assignment and have a week to revise and edit it. If they complete it, they are allowed to join the celebration. I don't tell them this until after the year-end writing test.)

I then ease their minds by telling them that they will be given a "practice test" each month that will help them see what kind of progress they are making. This also helps me keep track of their progress throughout the year. I have found that the promise of a celebration keeps the students' motivation high during writing class and the practice tests.

Alternative Rubric

The assessment used in the previous section is based on a six point rubric. I used this rubric successfully for more than ten years until California began using a four point rubric on its state writing exams. Suddenly, school districts across the state wanted teachers to use a four point rubric when scoring classroom writing assignments. Because of this change, I was forced to adjust my rubric to a four point scale.

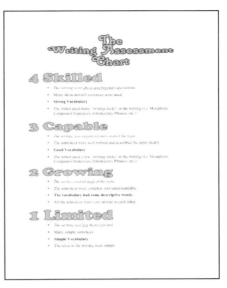

The next page contains the new four point rubric shown here. Personally, I prefer the six point rubric. It is much more specific, and it is easier for the students to show growth. On a four point rubric, students needs to improve considerably before their improvements translate to higher scores.

With this new rubric, the students would look at the 3 "Capable" when they begin the assessment. The 4 would be reserved for "above and beyond" work, while the 2 would be approaching grade level ability.

Alternative Assessment Sheets

To simplify the assessment process, the alternate assessment sheet shown here combines the Writing Assessment Chart (rubric) with the Writing Assessment Sheet. On one sheet (printed back-to-back) the students can see all five assessment items and the bullet points used in the assessments.

The students can simply follow along on the worksheet and assess the writing without the use of the Writing Assessment Checklist and the Writing Assessment Chart. Here, they can write the scores in the boxes and an explanation of the scores on the lines below. It makes the student conferences run more smoothly as well.

Another way to make this new assessment sheet even more powerful is to make a separate assessment sheet for narrative and expository writing. The following pages contain two scoring sheets – one for narrative assignments and the other for expository assignments. As you read the bullet points under each item, you will notice that each assessment item is tailored specifically to each type of writing. Both of these new assessment sheets have become powerful tools in my writing program.

4 Skilled

- *The writing went <u>above and beyond</u> expectations*
- Many show-not-tell sentences were used.
- **Strong Vocabulary**
- The writer used many "writing tricks" in the writing (i.e. Metaphors, Compound Sentences, Introductory Phrases, etc.)

3 Capable

- *The writing was organized and covered the topic.*
- The sentences were well written and described the topic clearly.
- **Good Vocabulary**
- The writer used a few "writing tricks" in the writing (i.e. Metaphors, Compound Sentences, Introductory Phrases, etc.)

2 Growing

- *The writer covered <u>most</u> of the topic.*
- The sentences were complete and understandable.
- **The vocabulary had some descriptive words.**
- All the sentences were very similar to each other.

1 Limited

- *The writing was <u>less</u> than expected.*
- Many simple sentences.
- **Simple Vocabulary**
- The ideas in the writing were simple.

Author's Name: _____   Editor's Name: _____

Writing Assessment Sheet

Type of writing being assessed: _____

Instructions:

1. Read through the writing once. Edit by checking for spelling and punctuation errors.
2. Check the writing for the items listed below. In the box to the right, write the score that best describes the writing.
3. In the space below each section, explain why the writer received that score.

Narrative

1. The Writer Covered the Topic Completely

Score

4 – The writing went above and beyond expectations.

3 – All expected elements were included and done well.

2 – Some expected elements were included or done fairly well.

1 – Many of the elements were missing.

Explain the Score: _____

_____

_____

2. Show – Not–Tell

Score

4 – The many show–not–tell sentences helped me picture the story in my mind perfectly.

3 – Several show–not–tell sentences helped me picture the story in my mind very well.

2 – There were many good sentences, and I could picture some parts of the story.

1 – Many simple sentences were used creating a simple picture in my mind.

Explain the Score: _____

_____

_____

3. Vocabulary

4 – The writing had strong vocabulary.

3 – The writing had good vocabulary.

2 – The writing had some descriptive words.

1 – The writing had simple vocabulary.

Explain the Score: _____

_____

_____

4. Writing Tricks

Score

4 – The writer used many writing tricks.

3 – The writer used a few writing tricks.

2 – All the sentences were very similar to each other.

1 – The ideas in the writing were simple.

Explain the Score: _____

_____

_____

5. Overall, how did the writer do?

Score

4 – There were few spelling, punctuation, and grammatical errors.
It was a very entertaining story.

3 – There were some spelling, punctuation, and grammatical errors.
It was a good story.

2 – The spelling, punctuation, and grammatical errors made the story
difficult to understand. More details would have made the story better.

1 – The story was too difficult to read or understand.

Explain the Score: _____

_____

_____

Author's Name: _____   Editor's Name: _____

Writing Assessment Sheet

Type of writing being assessed: _____

Instructions:

1. Read through the writing once. Edit by checking for spelling and punctuation errors.
2. Check the writing for the items listed below. In the box on the right, write the score that best describes the writing.
3. In the space below each section, explain why the writer received that score.

Expository

1. The Writer Covered the Topic Completely

    4 – The writing went above and beyond expectations.

    3 – All expected elements were included and done well.

    2 – Some expected elements were included or done fairly well.

    1 – Many of the elements were missing.

Score

Explain the Score: _____

_____

_____

2. Show – Not–Tell / Supporting Sentences

    4 – Each paragraph had a strong topic sentence and strong supporting details.

    3 – Each paragraph had a good topic sentence and strong supporting details.

    2 – Most paragraphs were about one main idea.

    1 – More supporting sentences are needed to explain the topic.

Score

Explain the Score: _____

_____

_____

3. Vocabulary

4 – The writing had strong vocabulary.

3 – The writing had good vocabulary.

2 – The writing had some descriptive words.

1 – The writing had simple vocabulary.

Explain the Score: _____

_____

_____

4. Writing Tricks

Score

4 – The writer used many writing tricks.

3 – The writer used a few writing tricks.

2 – All the sentences were very similar to each other.

1 – The ideas in the writing were simple.

Explain the Score: _____

_____

_____

5. Overall, how did the writer do?

Score

4 – There were few spelling, punctuation, and grammatical errors.
   It was a very informative report.

3 – There were some spelling, punctuation, and grammatical errors.
   It was an informative report.

2 – The spelling, punctuation, and grammatical errors made the report
   difficult to understand. More details would have made the report better.

1 – The report was too difficult to read or understand.

Explain the Score: _____

_____

_____

I. Warmup

Sample Lesson Plan for Teaching
the Writing Assessment Program

Days 1 - 2

II.

A. Hand out the Writing Assessment Checklist, Writing Assessment Chart, and the Assessment Sheet. Begin by explaining to the students that they are going to learn how to grade* each other's writing using these three papers. Some will catch on right away and others will need a little time.

B. Explain what this program will do for them. It will:
    1. Help them know exactly what it takes to be a great writer.
    2. Take all the guess work out of revising and editing their writing.
    3. Help them intelligently grade* other people's writing as well as their own.
  * I use the word <u>grade</u> for now until they understand assessment.

C. Give the students three to five minutes to read the Writing Assessment Checklist. Have them read it several times. Tell them to use this time to start memorizing the five items. By the end of the week they will take a test in which they will have to write the five items on this checklist. When finished, ask the class if anyone can name an item on the list without looking.

D. Review the 5 items of the Writing Assessment Checklist with the students. (Approx. 20 minutes)
    1. Ask them to give possible reasons why these items will help improve their writing.
    2. Review each of the 5 items of the Writing Assessment Checklist. Have them read each item as a class before you explain it. Emphasize how each part will make them better writers, and they will be using this to grade* each other's writing.

III.

E. Assess the writing sample, Paragraph #1, from the appendix together. (15 min.)*

F. Assess the writing sample, Paragraph #2, from the appendix together. (15 min.)*
  * Most elementary students will need the Writing Assessment Conversion Chart (See Appendix) to help them do the division.

G. Show how improving in each area improves the total writing score.

** While teaching this part of the writing program, begin each day by reviewing the five items of the Writing Assessment Checklist. Ask them to memorize the checklist as homework. Then, each day, have the students race to see who can say the five items the fastest. (The record for my class is 3.13 seconds.)

Days 3 - 5

Give the students small writing assignments (or use writing samples from the Appendix) for them to assess using the Writing Assessment Checklist. They should assess writing samples as many times as it takes to get comfortable with the process.

By assessing each others' writing, they reinforce what it takes to be a great writer. They are also learning to make judgments about writing that they will apply to their own writing. Assessing in this way allows students to see examples of their peers' writing, and creates opportunities for peer tutoring.

Days 3-5 is a great time to reinforce the following:
1. The difference between grades and assessment.
2. How improvement in one of the items also improves the other items.
   (i.e… Improving vocabulary also helps show-not-tell sentences, etc.)
3. While they are assessing, <u>they</u> are the teacher. Any score they give is okay as long as they can defend it using the Writing Assessment Chart.

Monthly
   * Work on pre-writing and other ways to make sure students "**<u>write everything</u>** they are assigned to write" while reinforcing paragraph and essay writing. (See Ch. 2)
   * Teach 2 or more **<u>show-not-tell</u>** concepts a month. (See Ch. 3)
   * Teach **<u>vocabulary</u>** units. (See Ch. 4)
   * Teach 2 or more **<u>writing tricks</u>**. (See Ch. 5)

   ** The second or third month is a good time to give the students writing goals.

End of the Year.
   * End of the year assessment and celebration for attaining writing goals.
   * Create a make up assignment for those who didn't reach their writing goal.

Chapter 2
Helping Students Write Everything They Are Expected to Write

This chapter will:

1. Help students cover all the details they are expected to include in their writing.

2. Help students organize their thoughts before writing.

3. Help home school parents understand what is expected at each grade level.

4. Provide writing samples for home school parents to use as a guide to compare with their children's writing.

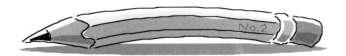

Pre-Writing

One of the best ways to get students to write <u>everything they are expected</u> to write is **pre-writing**. Here is the definition I have my students repeat when we review the writing process:

"Putting your ideas on paper so you don't get brain-block."

Many of my students are so anxious to get started on writing assignments and writing tests, they don't want to take the time to pre-write. They have good ideas in mind and want to charge ahead. However, they fail to realize that they will need several good ideas that are well organized to fulfill the requirement of writing everything they are expected to write. Consequently, they will use phrases in their writing such as, "Oh, I forgot to say that..." or, "P.S. before all this happened..."

Before your students begin a writing assignment, review the writing process with an emphasis on pre-writing. Nag your students. Constantly remind them that if they do a good job of pre-writing, actually writing the assignment will be a piece of cake. Say something like:

"How many times have you been working on an assignment, and you couldn't figure out what to say? Or, you knew what you wanted to say, but you couldn't put it into words? This is called brain-block, and, if you pre-write, this happens less frequently. Prewriting helps you spend your writing time sounding intelligent rather than searching for what to say."

It's true that if you put your ideas down on paper, your writing will have better organization and will show more intelligence. There are thousands of great pre-writing techniques, and the concept is not difficult to figure out. Here are some ways to use pre-writing to assure that students completely meet the reader's expectations. Feel free to adjust the ideas to fit the specific needs of your students.

Essay and Prompt Writing

If your students are familiar with the Writing Assessment Checklist, now is a good time to remind them that pre-writing is the best way to make sure they get a good score on the first item on the checklist. This will motivate many of them.

Remember the definition of pre-writing: "Putting your ideas on paper so you don't get brain-block." Keep pre-writing that simple.

When students are given a writing assignment, the expectations should be clearly defined. Writing prompts generally do this very well. (See the Appendix for sample writing prompts.) Writing prompts typically spell out very clearly what the student is expected to write. Any other writing assignments should clearly state what is expected of the writer. In many cases, you may want to create simple instructions so students have the freedom to be creative. However, if you want them to write about something specific, and the expectations are not clear, don't be surprised when their content is not what you wanted.

<u>**Teach the students to do this:**</u>
1. **Underline or highlight the expectations in the assignment or prompt.**
2. **Decide how they will pre-write. (See below for ideas.)**
3. **List their ideas, and put a check mark on the assignment or prompt when they have listed facts related to that expectation.**
4. **Put the ideas in order.**

<u>Pre-Writing Techniques</u>

 Clustering

 Listing

Clustering

I like clustering because it gives you room to grow. If more ideas come to mind about a topic, you have room to add them to your pre-writing.

Here is a cluster.

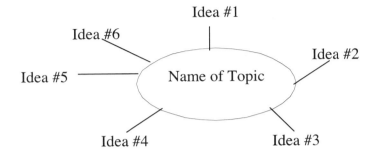

For <u>younger students</u> who are still learning how to write paragraphs, this is a good way to start. Let's say the students are asked to write a summary about a story you've read in class. How would they pre-write?

Prompt: Write a paragraph about the story of <u>David and Goliath</u>.

Step 1 - Underline or highlight the expectations.

Write a <mark>paragraph</mark> <mark>about</mark> the story of <mark>David and Goliath</mark>.

Step 2 - We've chosen the cluster, and now we will list ideas. The topic will go in the middle of the cluster. Use the top half of the paper for the cluster and the bottom half for the paragraph. This makes access to the cluster easier during writing.

David and Goliath

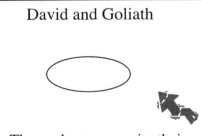

The students can write their paragraph here so they have easy access to the information in the cluster.

Step 3 - Make a list of ideas that would fit in a paragraph on that topic.

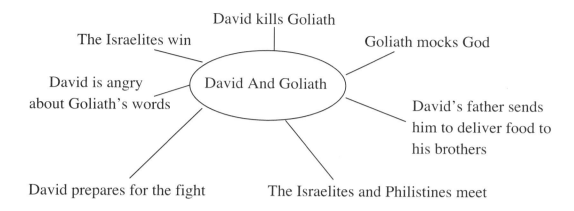

Note: The ideas in the cluster are <u>not</u> necessarily in complete sentences. The goal for the pre-writing is to get the ideas down on paper as quickly as possible. Words, phrases, or sentences are okay.

Step 4 - Teach the students to put the facts in sequential order. Have them number the facts from first to last.

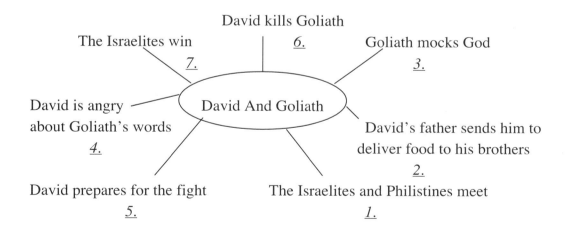

Now, the students are guaranteed that the main facts of the story will be represented in the paragraph. It will be well organized, and they will be free to work on the style of their writing rather than focusing strictly on the content of the paragraph.

The only difference for the <u>older students</u> is how they organize their clusters. Let's take the same topic, but apply it to the more experienced student.

Topic: Write an essay summarizing the story of David and Goliath.

Step 1 - Underline or highlight the expectations.

Topic: Write an <u>essay</u> <u>summarizing</u> the story of <u>David and Goliath</u>.

In this case, the assignment is an essay that requires several paragraphs. At this age, students should be able to identify the beginning, middle, and end of a story. To help them do this, they can organize their clusters in this way:

As with many essays, the students should begin by identifying three main ideas of the topic. In our example, the three main ideas would be the beginning, middle, and end of the story. I recommend that you have your students write "3 Main Ideas" at the top of all essays and stories followed by their list of the three main ideas. This will help them stay focused on the topic.

David and Goliath

3 Main Ideas:
1. The Israelites and Philistines face off.
2. David prepares for the fight.
3. Israel wins.

The Israelites and Philistines face off

David prepares for the fight

Israel wins

Once they have divided the summary into the three main ideas, follow the same pattern as steps 2- 4 in the previous example.

Keep in mind that each cluster is not limited to one paragraph. As ideas and information increase, clusters can become two or three paragraphs. Older students should be able to recognize when a new paragraph should begin and how to make smooth transitions.

Note: Older students should be required to produce essays that are more than mere summaries. There should be evidence of critical thinking (such as practical application or opinions about the topic.) For example, a more appropriate assignment might be: Summarize the story of David and Goliath and explain how this story can help people understand the character of God.

Listing

Listing is another form of pre-writing. It follows the same basic ideas as clustering except students make a list of the ideas that they want to include in their report. Depending on learning style, this may be an option that some students require. Every year I have students who need to list their pre-writing because they find the cluster too "cluttered." Here is how the previous clusters will look in the listed format:

<table>
<tr><td>

David and Goliath

1. David kills Goliath.
2. Goliath mocks God.
3. David's father sends him to deliver food to his brothers.
4. The Israelites and Philistines meet.
5. David prepares for the fight.
6. David is angry about Goliath's words.
7. The Israelites win.

</td><td>

David and Goliath

3 Main Ideas:
1. The Israelites and Philistines face off.
2. David prepares to fight.
3. Israel Wins.

The Israelites and Philistines face off.
1.
2.
3.
4.
5.

David prepares to fight.
1.
2.
3.
4.
5.

Israel Wins!
1.
2.
3.
4.
5.

</td></tr>
</table>

The worksheets on the following pages (right) are good teaching tools. They can help ease your students into the practice of pre-writing. After a few weeks, they will be able to create these prewriting formats on their own.

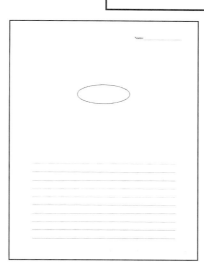
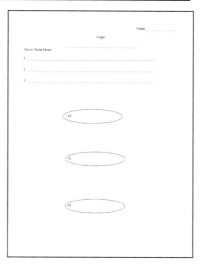

Name_____

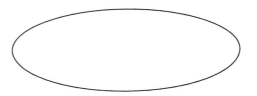

_____

_____

_____

_____

_____

_____

_____

_____

_____

_____

Topic

_____

Three Main Ideas:

1. _____

2. _____

3. _____

Grade-by-Grade Expectations - What should they know by now?

As I wrote in the preface, when I first started teaching, I had no idea what my seventh graders should know coming into my class, and what they should know when they left. Fortunately, I was able to find a district curriculum guide to help me along. Here is a summary of what your students should be able to do by the end of each grade. Use it to help you assess student writing on the Writing Assessment Checklist.

3rd Grade Expectations

1. Know the parts of a sentence.
2. Write many complete sentences together without fragment or run-on sentences.
3. Be able to write basic paragraphs.
4. Understand when one paragraph ends and the next begins.
5. Be able to write multiple paragraphs about one topic.
6. Be able to do simple pre-writes and first drafts on writing topics.
7. First drafts should show some kind of logical organization.
8. Have an understanding of the parts of speech, especially nouns, verbs, and adjectives.

3rd grade writing samples:

Average   High

No More Crime	No More Crime
The world would be a better place if there were no more crime and violence. People would be happy and safe. They would not fight all the time. If there weren't any crime and violence people wouldn't get hurt all the time. People wouldn't be scared to walk in the street. That's what I think, don't you?	If we all worked together, there would be no more crime in the world. Instead of guns and knives, there would be handshakes and hugs. All races would get along, and we would live in peace and harmony. Everybody would laugh and talk to each other instead of cry because someone was murdered. It doesn't matter if you are black, white, Mexican, or any other race. We should all get along. This is what would happen if we all got along.

4th Grade Expectations

1. Be able to write a variety of sentences such as simple and compound sentences.
2. Have a firm understanding of a paragraph: Be able to write a topic sentence, supporting sentences, closing sentence, and know to start a new paragraph when starting a new main idea.
3. Begin essay writing. The three-paragraph essay should be introduced, if not mastered.
4. Be able to write a well organized essay to a writing topic in a timed situation.
5. Be able to revise and edit their own writing to produce a final draft.
6. Be able to state an opinion and defend it.
7. A clear writing style should be developing by this time which includes a variety of writing techniques such as dialogue, similes/metaphors, attention getters.
8. Writing should begin to reflect the author's knowledge of the audience. (For example, if the writing is directed to the President, it should reflect the proper respect.)
9. Knowledge of the parts of speech including nouns, verbs, adjectives, pronouns, adverbs, and prepositions.
10. Have basic research skills.

4th grade writing samples:

Average

My Holiday Wish

My holiday wish for the world is for gangs to stop committing crimes in our cities. They put graffiti on the walls and make people say, "Our city is ugly." They also commit felonies like shooting people and taking drugs. This makes the crime worse and makes people sad. If we don't do something about this problem, our world will be a bad place to live.

There are many things we can do to help stop gangs. If students listen to their teachers and do well in school, they will get good grades and not need gangs. We can help clean up the graffiti whenever we see it. When we see a poor, sad kid we could be a friend so he won't need gangs. Also, we could say no to drugs.

Our world would be a better place if we didn't have gangs. Children could go outside and play without being afraid. We could hang out at the mall and not get bullied. If there were not gangs, we would all be safer.

High

My Holiday Wish

My holiday wish for the world is that people would recycle so the world would be a nice, more beautiful place to live. Can you imagine all the sodas, juices and drinks that Americans drink every day? If every one of those cans and bottles were recycled, we would have a much cleaner planet. Look at all the newspapers that are made everyday. Think of all the tall, beautiful trees we could save if every newspaper was recycled. We should all be like busy little beavers and do our part to help clean up the world by recycling.

I'm going to do my part to help my wish come true. First, I'm going to make a space in my back yard for aluminum cans and a space for newspapers. Once my family is recycling, I'm going to talk my neighbors into saving their stuff for me. "Pleeeeeease, can I have your cans and newspapers," I ask while flapping my big, brown eyes. They'll be putty in my hands. By doing my part and encouraging others to do their part, my wish for a clean world will come true.

Making my wish come true will take more than just a few chores around the house. I will recruit family, friends, and even the community to help recycle. My parents can do their part by helping organize a recycle program at work. My friends and I can ask local restaurants to use paper containers instead of Styrofoam. Finally, wastebaskets at thousands of schools across the country are packed with paper. Recycling all of this paper would be a great way to help make my holiday wish come true.

5th Grade Expectations

1. Be able to write a variety of sentences such as simple, compound, and complex sentences.
2. Write essays with a basic understanding of introduction and conclusion paragraphs.
3. Be able to follow the writing process from pre-writing to publishing on their own.
4. Be able to write a narrative that includes all the elements of a story including setting, conflict, climax, rising action, resolution, and epilogue.
5. Be able to research a topic and write an intelligent, well organized essay which demonstrates an understanding of the topic.
6. A clear understanding of the audience should be present.
7. Knowledge of the parts of speech should be reflected in their writing. Use of adverbs and prepositional phrases to enhance writing should be used.
8. At ease in all domains of writing.

5th grade writing samples:

Average

One Great Week

Until this day, I still dream about the time that my friend Brad came to visit me from his far away home in Florida. I can still remember how much fun we had on his one-week trip. His parents were going to Europe, and they wanted us to let him stay for awhile. As he walked off the airplane, he had a spark in his eyes as if to say, "Let's have some fun." I gave him a nod, and we both smiled.

That night we slept in sleeping bags on the floor and stayed up late to play games and watch television. The next morning, we went to the movies and then in the afternoon, we ate pizza, hamburgers, and sodas. We were so full of food that we both took naps, something that Brad and I hated to do. Then at night, we were informed by my parents to go to sleep early because the next day we were going to Disneyland!

The next day we woke up early. We were told we could be trusted alone so my Mom gave me some money and told us that whenever we got there, we could go wherever we wanted. Later, when we got to Disneyland, I grabbed Brad's hand and headed for Splash Mountain. By the time the day was over, we had gone on every ride in the park, even the baby rides.

The rest of the week, we stayed at home and played games while watching cartoons. When it was time for Brad to leave, I decided that this was the best time I'd ever had.

High

One Great Week

Until this day, I still dream about the time that my friend Brad came to visit me from his far away home in Florida. He had moved away three months before, and I thought I'd never see him again. The knot in my stomach felt like a rock when he left. "Honey, Brad's parents are going to Europe for a week, and they want to know if Brad can stay here. Is that okay?" my mom asked. She took it as a yes when I bounced around the room like a ping-pong ball while screaming my head off. Now he was coming back, and I couldn't wait. We were going to have the time of our lives.

As he walked off the airplane, he had a spark in his eyes as if to say, "Let's have some fun." I gave him a nod and we both smiled. We began our adventure that night. We stayed up late to play games and watch TV and slept in sleeping bags on the floor.

The next morning, we went to the movies and then in the afternoon, we ate pizza, hamburgers, and sodas. We were so full of food that we both took naps, something that Brad and I hated to do. "You guys might want to go to bed early tonight," my dad said casually. "Why?" I asked, suspecting that something might be going on. "Well, tomorrow I thought it might be fun to go to Disneyland." Brad and I looked at each other, slapped our hands over our face and screamed our heads off.

The next day we woke up at 6:00 AM sharp and made so much noise my parents HAD to get up. We were told we could be trusted alone so my Mom gave me some money and told us that whenever we got there, we could go wherever we wanted. Later, when we got to Disneyland I grabbed Brad's hand and headed for Splash Mountain. By the time the day was over, we had gone on every ride in the park, even the baby rides.

The rest of the week, we stayed at home and played games while watching cartoons. On Saturday, it was time for Brad to leave, but our goodbye wasn't a sad one this time. We both knew that his mom and dad loved to travel, which meant more visits from him. There was no doubt that this was the best time I'd ever had.

6th Grade Expectations

1. See 5th grade expectations.
2. Mastery of the five-paragraph essay.
3. Grammar and spelling errors should be minimal on first drafts, nonexistent on final drafts.
4. Research papers should show thorough knowledge of the topic as well as critical thinking about the relevance of the topic.
5. Student's writing voice and style should be clearly present.

* 6th grade writing samples:

Average

Advice for a New Kid at School

As a new student at our school, you might have a few problems getting adjusted. I am going to help you get through this awkward, beginning phase and help you solve some problems you might have.

One problem you might have right away is people calling you names. When people say things like, "Hey, look who's here. It's Banana Brain!" don't burst into tears and hang your head low. Just ignore them or tell the teacher. Don't punch them or start a fight because you don't want to get into trouble in your first week of school.

Another problem you will have is that you won't have many friends. Now you're probably asking, "How do I get friends?" Well, to get friends you have to have a nice attitude. Also, sharing is a good way to get to know people. Before you know it you'll be trading things like necklaces, bracelets, pencils, erasers, and even some toys. However, if it takes longer to make friends than it should, cheer up, you've still got one friend, ME.

Finally, you might find yourself having a problem making friends because you develop a teasing habit. Believe me, you don't want to tease. Some people start doing it because they think they're being cool. Ask yourself, how does it feel to be teased? If you find yourself developing this habit, stop it immediately.

If you follow this advice I've given you, you should have no problems adjusting to our wonderful school. There are terrific people here who would love to be your friend if you just give them a chance.

Advice for a New Kid at School

So you're a new student in school, and you're having a few problems getting adjusted to your new environment, huh? Well, that's to be expected. It just takes some people more time than others to fit in, but I assure you, if you take my advice you'll fit right in.

First of all, you can't let yourself become intimidated by all your short-comings. Expect to be teased, but when it happens, don't over react. Play along with it like it's no big deal. It might help to even play along. If your braces are the target of the day, laugh it off and say, "These will be gone next year, but your teeth will still be yellow." If you're still alive, you've probably become one of the crowd. Kids our age love a good put down.

Next, you might have a problem with people calling you names. When people call to you and say, "Hey, look who's here. It's Banana Brain!" don't burst into tears and hang your head low. This would be like putting a target on your back and handing everyone bows and arrows. The best thing to do is to smile and show them that you are a boring target.

Finally, once you've been accepted into the pack, don't start acting like the top dog. Remember, the nail that sticks out gets hammered down. You're still the new kid on the block, and if you develop an attitude, get used to hearing, "Who does this person think she is?" or "Go back to your home planet, weirdo!" Just be as nice as possible, and people will respect you for it. You'll find that once the kids here get to know you, life will be great.

Well, I hope this advice has been helpful. Just be sure to keep in mind all the wise words I've told you. Don't panic when you get teased because you know that's going to happen. Also, when people call you names, don't burst into tears. Lastly, once you've been accepted, stay a nice person. Good luck and have fun, Banana Brain! Just kidding.

7th Grade Expectations

1. See 6th grade expectations.
2. Mastery of the five paragraph essay with strong supporting sentences.
3. A well-developed vocabulary and vivid imagery should be present.

* Middle school writing samples:

Average

A character from literature that reminds me of myself is Billy from <u>Where the Red Fern Grows</u>. He has many of the same qualities that I have. First, he is a poor, country boy who has to work hard for the things that he wants. His family can't even afford to put shoes on his feet. While my family is not that poor, I do have to work hard if I want anything special. Next, Billy stands up for himself when people pick on him. I try not to let people push me around too. Finally, we both love our pets. These are the three biggest similarities between Billy and me.

Billy is a poor boy who lives in the hills of Oklahoma. When he sees something he wants, he goes after it with all his might and doesn't stop until he gets it. That is how he came to own these two great hunting dogs. He saves every penny he gets until he can afford Ann and Dan. When I want something, I am the same way. One time I wanted a special baseball bat. I collected aluminum cans, mowed lawns, and washed cars until I raised the $75. We both aren't rich, but when we see something we want, we go for it.

Another similarity between Billy and me is that we don't let bullies push us around. In the book, Billy is bullied into a raccoon hunting competition between him and a bunch of bullies. These kids cheat, but Billy still comes out on top. I've been picked on a few times by bullies, and I either stand up for myself or ignore them in a way that shows them they're not getting to me. So dealing with bullies is something Billy and I know a lot about.

A third similarity we have is that we've both had great pets. Billy trained his dogs ever since they were puppies. He played with them and took care of them in every way. At the end of the book, one of his dogs is killed trying to save his life. Billy is broken hearted, and I know exactly how he feels. My first dog, King, was the best dog a kid could have. We played at the parks and he pulled me on my skateboard. When he got sick, we had to put him to sleep. We both share a love for our pets.

The main character in <u>Where the Red Fern Grows</u> and I are very similar. I have to work hard if I want something, just like Billy. No one is going to give us anything. We both have had bad experiences with bullies, and we both have come out feeling good about ourselves at the end. Finally, we both have had good, loyal pets. We will keep our pets alive in our memories for the rest of our lives. This book was much better because the main character reminded me so much of myself.

"Whoop! Whoop!" he shouts to his two hunting dogs, Ann and Dan, as he chases after them, fresh on the trail of a raccoon. He finally catches up to them as they dance around the tree howling at their cornered prize. Through the branches he sees his trophy and brings it down with one shot of his old rifle. This boy, nearly a man, is the protagonist in the wonderful book <u>Where the Red Fern Grows</u>. He is a character from literature that reminds me of myself. Although we live in different eras in time and different areas of the world, there are so many things we have in common.

Billy is a poor boy who lives in the Ozark hills of Oklahoma. When he sees something he wants, he goes after it with all his might and doesn't stop until he gets it. That is how he came to own these two great hunting dogs. He saves every penny he gets until he can afford Ann and Dan. When I want something I am the same way. One time I wanted a special thirty-three inch, twenty-nine ounce baseball bat. It was the perfect bat for me. I went door to door collecting aluminum cans, mowed a dozen lawns, and washed a fleet of cars until I raised the $75. We both aren't rich, but when we see something we want, we go for it.

Another quality we both share is that we don't let bullies push us around. In the book, Billy is bothered by a family of children, known throughout the county for being rotten. He finds himself duped into a competition with these kids and is forced to have Ann and Dan try to catch more raccoons than the bullies' dogs. Of course these kids cheat, but Billy still comes out on top. I've been beat up a few times because I've stood up to bullies, but at least now they know that if they want to pick on me, they're not going to have an easy time of it. This is a quality both Billy and I share.

A third quality that we share is how much we care for our pets. From the time they were pups, Billy spent all of his time with his dogs. He trained them, played with them, and took care of them in every way. At the end of the book, one of his dogs is killed trying to save his life. Billy is devastated. I know exactly how he feels. My first dog, King, went everywhere with me. He'd known me since I was born and he looked out for me. When I was old enough, we played at the parks and he pulled me on my skateboard. When he got sick we had to put him down. Like Billy, I was devastated. We both share a love for our pets.

I was able to enjoy the book <u>Where the Red Fern Grows</u> because I knew exactly how the main character felt. I have to work hard if I want something, just like Billy. No one is going to give us anything. We both have had bad experiences with bullies, and we both have come out feeling good about ourselves at the end. Finally, we both have had good, loyal pets. We will keep our pets alive in our memories for the rest of our lives. I was able to enjoy this book much better because the main character reminded me so much of myself.

Chapter 3
Helping Students Write Sentences That Show, Not Tell

This chapter will:

1. Help students write descriptive sentences that paint pictures with their words.

2. Provide the teacher with lesson plans for teaching several show-not-tell concepts.

3. Teach students how to expand their writing beyond the who, what, where, when, and how.

Show-Not-Tell

Are you tired of your students using only a few general sentences to describe a topic that needs more explanation? This is why I started teaching students to show, not tell. It began when my fourth grade students would write: "I got a video game for Christmas. I was excited." Instead of **telling** their reader what they got and how they felt, the students had to **show** the reader what they got and how they felt. Their new sentences would read something like this: " I tore through the wrapping paper like piranha attacking a piece of meat. It was the new Sega video game that I've wanted for months. My eyes grew as big as the moon. I jumped ten feet into the air while screaming my head off. I threw myself into my parents' arms, sending them rolling on the ground."

If you think the example above is sophisticated for fourth graders, try some of these lessons with your class. You might be surprised. Seeing the success of the first show-not-tell lessons, I began to create other lessons to help students become more descriptive in their writing.

The ideas in this section have been tremendously successful and highly motivating for the students. When I finish the introductions to many of these lessons, several of my students each year are literally yelling at me to let them start writing. I will explain the concept to you as I explain it to my students. You may use this as a sample lesson plan or adjust it to fit your curriculum. I hope you have as much fun with this as I've had.

What is Show-Not-Tell?

This is how I explain it to my students. Feel free to use any part of it to help your students understand this concept.

Sample
Lesson Plan

"The words you use when you write should help paint a picture in your readers' minds. Your readers should see in their minds what you are talking about as if they are watching a movie. This is SHOW. Here are two stories. Which one is SHOW, and which one is TELL?

1. There was a car accident at the corner yesterday.

Could you see in your mind what happened? No! It was boring because I just TOLD you what happened.

2. (With energy) Yesterday I was crossing the street and I heard the squeal of tires racing around the corner. A red Camero with tinted windows was flying right at me. I dove into the gutter while it banked a hard left, bounced off a tree, and plowed right into a fire hydrant. A

giant spray of water gushed fifty feet into the air, drenching about twenty kids who stared in shock with blank expressions on their dripping faces at the wreckage in front of them. What a sight!

> Could you see in your mind what happened? Yes! I SHOWED you what happened. I didn't just TELL you, 'There was a car accident yesterday.' I am going to show you how to paint pictures with your words. I am going to teach you how to show, not tell."

Now, I repeat the definition of show-not-tell with them:

> "Before we go any further, let's repeat the definition of show-not-tell together: 'We show what is happening by painting a picture with our words, not just telling what is happening.'"

Note: Every time you teach a show-not-tell concept, have your students review the definition of show-not-tell. Have them pretend that their pencils are paintbrushes. The students wave their "paint brushes" in the air (as if they are painting) and say, "Show-not-tell is painting a picture with words."

Teaching a Show-Not-Tell Lesson

After going over the introduction, teach any of the show-not-tell lessons on the following pages. After the first lesson, whenever you teach a show-not-tell lesson, begin by reviewing the five parts of the Writing Assessment Checklist. Concentrate on #2: "Did the writer use Show-Not-Tell sentences?" These lessons will make this score improve dramatically. (This really encourages the highly motivated students.)

Writing Assessment Checklist

1. Did the writer completely cover the topic?
2. Did the writer use Show-Not-Tell sentences?
3. How is the writer's vocabulary?
4. Did the writer use Writing Tricks?
5. Overall, how did the writer do?

Also, when you have the students revise their writing, require that they add or change sentences so that they become show-not-tell sentences.

It is a great idea to have your students keep these lessons in a writing folder. They can use the worksheets for reference when they work on writing assignments, for review when they get rusty, and for journal practice when you want them to stay fresh. (More on this in Ch. 7 Putting It All Together.)

Show-Not-Tell Lessons
and Summaries

1. **Show-Not-Tell**

   Overview .... The Overview is the first page in my students' writing folders. They use it as a quick reference for all the show-not-tell concepts we learn. You can use this as your first lesson to introduce your students to the concept, or jump ahead to other lessons. I will be teaching more detailed lessons on most of the topics on this worksheet, so this page will work as a review later when the students begin to perfect the show-not-tell techniques presented here.

2. **Show-Not-Tell**

   Emotions .... These lessons always elicit great reactions from the students. They get to act out emotions and write about kid friendly topics. Also, they give the students dozens of ideas on how to paint pictures with words on very common ideas.

   A. Excited
   B. Scared
   C. Angry
   D. Sad

3. **Show-Not-Tell**

   Setting .... Great stories, as well as research papers, should give the reader a good sense of the setting. These lessons show the students how to give the reader a visual idea about where stories take place. Also, these skills help students involve the reader in the story.

4. **Show-Not-Tell**

   Poems .... This section provides poem formats to help your students practice show-not-tell techniques. Some of the poems are stories, some are settings, and some allow students to express their feelings.

5. **Show-Not-Tell**

   Words .... This section includes a list of show-not-tell words for sight, sound, touch, taste, and smell as well as better words for "said." These word lists serve as warm-ups for journal writing and are a resource for the students when they write stories.

   There is also a list of "dead words." These are words that are over-used by many students. I encourage the students to use the word lists to find more creative ways of expressing themselves.

Show-Not-Tell
Overview

How to present this lesson:

Materials:
Writing Assessment Checklist, Show-Not-Tell Overview worksheet, Show-Not-Tell Paragraph
Review worksheet, chalkboard.

① Review the Writing Assessment Checklist. Emphasize that this lesson will improve #2 on the checklist.

② Review the definition of show-not-tell:
"We show what is happening by <u>painting a picture with our words</u>, <u>not just telling</u> what happened."

③ Have the students look at the Show-Not-Tell Overview worksheet. Go over each tell phrase and make a list on the chalkboard of the ideas they create. Three or four ideas for each is plenty. Use the Show Phrase samples on the right-hand side to help guide them to the ideas. When finished, select one phrase as a class sample and put it on the review sheet below the samples given.

④ Go over the Show-Not-Tell Paragraph worksheet. Explain th̲a̲t̲ ̲t̲h̲i̲s̲ ̲i̲s̲ ̲a̲ ̲s̲t̲o̲r̲y̲ ̲w̲h̲e̲r̲e̲ ̲t̲h̲e̲ ̲s̲h̲o̲w̲-̲n̲o̲t̲-̲t̲e̲l̲l̲ ̲p̲h̲r̲a̲s̲e̲s̲ ̲h̲a̲v̲e̲ ̲b̲e̲e̲n̲ ̲l̲e̲f̲t̲ ̲o̲u̲t̲. Have them fill in the blanks with the phrases from the Overview worksheet that fit the best. I suggest you do the first two with them. Reluctant or insecure students may need assurance that they are doing it correctly. Make yourself available to explain what types of phrases would fit in each blank. Suggest some phrases. When I do this, I do not let them copy the suggestions that I make. They must think of their own. *Homework*

Here is an example:

In my room __*(along the wall, under the bed)*__ our little puppy was nervously hiding. Frightened by the fireworks, the ___*(hair on his neck stood straight up and he shivered frantically)*___. Kimmie and I looked at each other with sadness. ___*(We were ready to cry.)*___ We couldn't stand to see our helpless puppy suffer. ___*(With tears in our eyes)*___ we wondered what we could do to make Buddy feel better. "I know what we could do!" yelled Kimmie excitedly as ___*(a huge smile came over her face)*___. "We'll take Buddy to the park where there are no fireworks," she said ___*(dancing with excitement.)*___

As we arrived at the park, a band was playing ___*(among the giant pine trees)*___. We let Buddy run around and sniff the flowers ___*(that circled the playground)*___. In the sky we could see fireworks ___*(blasting between the stars)*___, but Buddy was having too much fun to notice. Suddenly, a teenager set off a package of firecrackers, and Buddy went crazy. ___*(He shivered and wailed with all of his might.)*___ I glared at Kimmie, ___*(my face turning bright red)*___, and said, "Don't they know fireworks are illegal in the park." By now we both felt so angry we ___*(screamed with fury)*___. In the end, we decided to go home and hold Buddy until the fireworks were over. Knowing we had tried our best to comfort Buddy made us feel much better.

Show-Not-Tell
Paragraph Review

In my room _____ our little

puppy was nervously hiding.   Frightened by the fireworks, the _____

_____. Kimmie and I looked at each other

with sadness. _____.

We couldn't stand to see our helpless puppy suffer. _____

_____ we

wondered what we could do to make Buddy feel better. "I know what

we can do!" yelled Kimmie excitedly as _____

_____. "We'll take Buddy to the park where there are no fireworks,"

she said _____.

  As we arrived at the park, a band was playing _____

_____. We let Buddy

run around and sniff the flowers _____

_____. In the sky we could see fireworks _____

_____, but Buddy was having too much fun to notice. Suddenly, a

teenager set off a package of firecrackers and Buddy went crazy.

_____. I glared at

Kimmie, _____

and said, "Don't they know fireworks are illegal in the park?" By

now we both felt so angry we _____

_____. In the end, we decided to go home and

hold Buddy until the fireworks were over. Knowing we had tried our best to

comfort Buddy made us feel much better.

Show-Not-Tell Overview

		Tell Phrase	**Show Phrase**
E m o t i o n s	EXCITED	He was excited.	gave a high five / jumped twenty feet into the air / _____
	SAD	They were sad.	tears formed in their eyes / bottom lip trembled / _____
	SCARED	They were scared.	teeth chattered / hair on his neck stood straight up / _____
	ANGRY	She was angry.	face turned bright red / clenched her fists / screamed with fury / _____

Tell Phrase	**Show Phrase**	**S e t t i n g**
In my room	along the wall / under the bed / between the covers / _____ _____	
In the sky	among the clouds / below the stars / _____ _____	
In the park	throught the trees / in the middle of the pond / _____ _____	

Show-Not-Tell
Emotions

How to present these lessons: This format will work for all 4 lessons.

Materials:

Everyone needs a piece of paper and pencil. Each student must draw a circle (cluster) in the middle of the sheet of paper with the name of the emotion in the middle. Draw a circle on a large piece of butcher paper with the emotion in the middle that will be used as a model. Make sure the butcher paper is at a level where the students can write on it with a marker.

1. Review the Writing Assessment Checklist. Emphasize that this lesson will improve #2 on the checklist.

2. Review the definition of <u>show-not-tell</u>: *on flash card*
   Holding up their pencils like a paintbrush - "We show what is happening by <u>painting a picture with our words</u>, <u>not just telling</u> what happened."

3. Have a student act out, in front of the class, the emotion you are learning. The others are to write three things they saw him/her do or say.

* Note: Some actors will need "motivation" to help them act. If acting out the emotion "excited" I might say, "You just hit the game-winning home run. Be excited! Go!" This will help bring out the emotion.

4. Select a few students to write a response on the butcher paper. Ask other students to volunteer their responses, and add them to the butcher paper. Everyone copies any answers that are written on the butcher paper.

** Repeat steps 3 and 4 two times. If you have some good ideas for that emotion, add them to the cluster. As the second and third actors finish performing, you can have the students write their responses on the board. I keep the cluster up on the bulletin board for several days for students to use as a reference.

5. Review the items on the cluster. These are ways that you can show, not tell that emotion. Isn't "tears rolled down my cheek" better than "I was sad" or "I cried." To show students how easily they can write descriptive sentences, compose several sentences using the ideas in the cluster. This allows them to hear how descriptive sentences should sound. (This is a very important step because verbal modeling is crucial. It gives the students confidence that their writing is acceptable.)

6. Prepare them for the story. Explain that you will tell them a story that will end at an emotional moment. Stress the fact that they will write how they _feel_. Obviously, they are going to feel the emotion simulated in the story. Be sure to tell them NOT to finish the story. Many of my students are so worked-up by this part of the story, they just write and write and write. Tell them to write only one paragraph showing, not telling the emotion.

next page

7. Read or tell them the story. BE DRAMATIC. Your students will really become involved in the story if you use a lot of emotion yourself.

8. **Immediately** after stopping the story, say "How do you feel? Write it!!!!!!!!" As they begin to write, remind them NOT to finish the story. They are to write only one paragraph using the ideas in the cluster. Give them writing ideas by calling out sentences from the cluster that might fit. Some will copy yours and some won't. This gives the slower students some ideas and models the process for the class.

9. Have students share their paragraphs with the class. (If time permits, have them read their paragraphs to each other in groups of four. This only takes a few minutes.) Students who finish early are allowed to illustrate their paragraph on "book paper." - (See Appendix)

** Be sure to have the students save their clusters in their writing folders for reference. I give homework assignments to follow-up and practice these skills. Also, I require a show-not-tell element in all of their writing so they need this as a reference.

Lesson Extensions

10. Collect and edit the paragraphs, or have the students edit each other's paragraphs. They can write and illustrate the final copy.

11. Have the students write the entire story you told them. They can insert this show-not-tell paragraph where it belongs. Also, they can now finish the story. See the Beyond the Lesson section at the end of each show-not-tell lesson.

12. After the stories are edited, you can combine them to make a book.

Show-Not-Tell
Excited

After acting out the emotion, here is a cluster my students created.

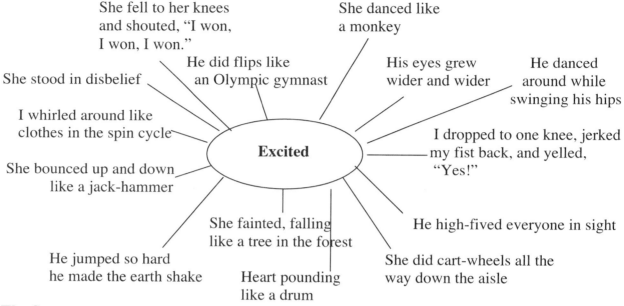

The Story

You're at Toys-R-Us with your mom, looking for a birthday present for your cousin, Michael. Wandering up and down the aisle, you drool over all the great stuff they have here: the Nintendos, the video games, the racing bikes, the athletic equipment. You know better than to ask your mom for anything. You can hear it now, "We're not here for you; we're here for Michael."

Suddenly, you notice it. Out of the corner of your eye you see a poster. "ONE HOUR FREE SHOPPING SPREE - Sign up here." You wander over to the display and read what it says. "The winner of this drawing will get to keep everything he or she can carry out of the store in one hour." "WOW, I've got to win this contest," you whisper as you nervously begin to fill out the card. With each letter you write, your confidence starts to grow. You KNOW that you will win this contest.

You show the poster to your mom and she splashes a dose of reality on the situation. "Look at all those cards, honey. Your chances of winning aren't very good." You look at the barrel full of cards. There are thousands of them. Still, somewhere deep in your heart, you know you have a chance to win.

After promising to do all your homework and chores for the week, your mom finally agrees to take you to the drawing which is this Saturday. All week you dream of the moment when they draw the winner. Each night as you go to sleep, you dream of yourself running up and down the aisles grabbing video games, baseball gloves, bikes, posters, candy, and much more. You even go to Toys-R-Us and plan your route, imagining what you will take first. The night before the drawing, you can't sleep. All you can do is toss and turn.

The morning finally arrives, and your mom pulls into the Toys-R-Us parking lot only to find hundreds of people standing around nervously. Up front, a barrel full of cards is on a stage. You know your card is inside that barrel, waiting to be pulled. A heavy-set man with a few skinny strands of hair covering his bald head approaches the microphone. News helicopters circle overhead as he thanks the crowd for coming.

"I will now draw the winning card for the one hour free shopping spree," he announces as every person in the crowd grabs their ticket. He reaches his chubby arm into the barrel and mixes the cards around. Your heart drops as several cards fall from the barrel. "Pick those up!!" you scream certain that one of those was yours. Your heart pounding, you stare as he pulls out the winning card.

"The winning number is ..."

You clasp your hands and look to the clouds saying, "Please let it be me."

"The first number is 4." You're in luck, your ticket number starts with 4. "The second number is 6." Your heart beats faster as you see that YOUR ticket says 4 6. "The third number is 9." You notice that your third number is 9 as the boy next to you rips his ticket crying, "That's not fair!" Only two more numbers left. The announcer looks at the card and calls "5." You hear girls crying, boys having tantrums, and you're afraid to look at your ticket. You find the courage to look. "Yes!" you shout. Your heart is racing a mile a minute. If he yells out 7, you're the winner. The man holds the ticket in his chubby fingers and calls out .....   "SEVEN!!!!!"

HOW DO YOU FEEL?
WRITE IT !!!!!!!!!

Beyond the Lesson

Have the students write the entire story using the writing tricks and show-not-tell words or phrases they've learned. Have them cluster each paragraph before they write. Break the story into five parts for them to make it easy to organize. Considering that they've already heard the story once, this part of the assignment shouldn't be too difficult. However, some students may need some coaching. Older students should be able to do this on their own.

Put this on the board, and cluster the first paragraph with them. The rest is up to them:

Paragraph #1
Entering the Contest

Paragraph #2
The Wait

Paragraph #3
The Big Day

Paragraph #4
The Show-Not-Tell
Excited Paragraph (Already Written)

Paragraph #5
The Shopping Spree

Show-Not-Tell
Scared

After acting out the emotion, here is a cluster my students created.

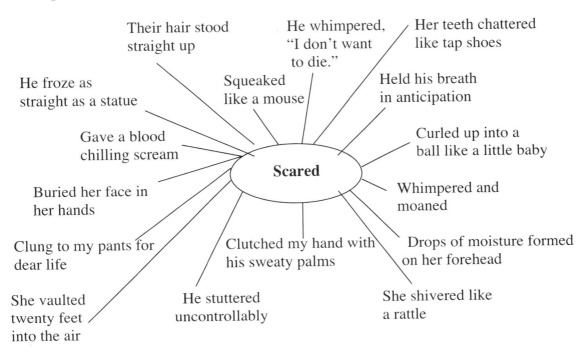

Their hair stood straight up

He whimpered, "I don't want to die."

Her teeth chattered like tap shoes

He froze as straight as a statue

Squeaked like a mouse

Held his breath in anticipation

Gave a blood chilling scream

Scared

Curled up into a ball like a little baby

Buried her face in her hands

Whimpered and moaned

Clung to my pants for dear life

Clutched my hand with his sweaty palms

Drops of moisture formed on her forehead

She vaulted twenty feet into the air

He stuttered uncontrollably

She shivered like a rattle

The Story

It's a cold November evening, and your parents are letting you stay home alone for the first time ever. You are totally excited. You're going to eat pizza until your stomach explodes, watch every scary movie that has ever been made, and stay up as late as your body will allow. It's going to be great!!!

As your parents get ready to leave, your mom kisses you on the forehead and says, "Be good; and be in bed by midnight." The door shuts behind them and you yell, "Yes, the house is mine!" while doing a crazy monkey dance around the living room. You put the first scary movie into the machine and sit down with a nice piece of pepperoni pizza.

By 11:00 that night you've had five pieces of pizza, a bag of chips, a gallon of soda, and you're watching your third horror movie, which is beginning to give you the creeps. The wind outside is starting to howl, the shutters are banging against the house, and the tree in the front yard is casting weird shadows through your living room window. The house is totally dark except for the glow of the TV showing a werewolf chase his victim. You look at your watch, starting to wish your parents would come home early.

Crack! "What was that?" you scream. Then you realize that it was PROBABLY the house settling. All of a sudden, you hear noises you've never heard before. Was that a branch tapping on the window, or is that a werewolf trying to get inside? Did I remember to lock the back door? "Stop it!" you tell yourself. "It's just your imagination." OR is it?

Certain that you're just imagining things, you turn off the movie and tune in to the Brady Bunch on Nick at Nite. But still, you can't shake the feeling that you're not alone in the house. Just to ease your mind, you decide to inspect the house. Lightning flashes, and suddenly raindrops start to splatter on the roof. First, you look into your room. You pause for a moment, listening for the sound of monster breathing. You yell, just in case someone IS there, "It's a good thing I've got this big knife." Another flash of lightning lights up your room, showing that there is no one there.

With the rain and wind punishing your house, you carefully inspect the kitchen, the bathroom, and finally the den. You feel a bit of relieved, then you freeze just outside your parents' bedroom. You stare inside, watching the rain blow in through the open window. You're certain that this window has been closed all night. Sheepishly you call out, "Is ... Is... Is anybody there?" BOOM! Thunder crashes above you as the spray from the window begins to drown the socks on your feet. "I'm being silly," you think to yourself. "I'll just go and shut the window and watch TV." However, the feeling that you're not alone is almost overwhelming. You take a baby step toward the window. Something moved in the corner of your eye, but it was just a shadow. "My parents will be home any minute now!" you shout just in case there IS and intruder hiding inside. Only three more steps and you're there. Two more steps. One more step. You reach out to grab the window and THUMP, a heavy hand falls on your shoulder!!!!!!!!!!!!!!!!!!!!!!!**

HOW DO YOU FEEL?
WRITE IT !!!!!!!!!

**Note: The students will be dying to know how the story ends. After they write their paragraphs, I tell them that it was all just an older brother's practical joke.

Beyond the Lesson

Have your students write the entire story using the writing tricks and show-not-tell they've learned. Ask them to cluster each paragraph before they write. Break the story into five parts for them to make it easy to organize. Considering that they've already heard the story once, this part of the assignment shouldn't be too difficult. However, some students may need some coaching. Older students should be able to do this on their own.

Put this on the board, and cluster the first paragraph with them. The rest is up to them:

Home Alone,
The House
Is Mine

Late Night,
Bad Weather

Home Inspection

Show-Not-Tell
Scared Paragraph
(Already Written)

The Hand

Show-Not-Tell
Angry

After acting out the emotion, here is a cluster my students created.

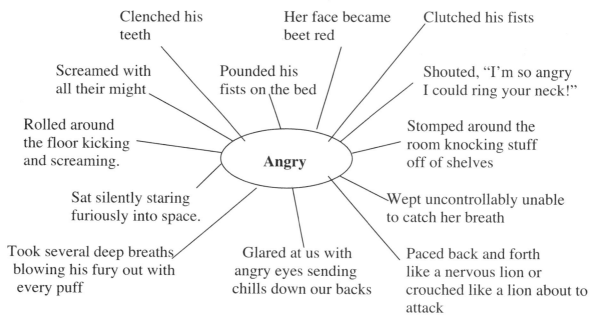

Clenched his teeth

Her face became beet red

Clutched his fists

Screamed with all their might

Pounded his fists on the bed

Shouted, "I'm so angry I could ring your neck!"

Rolled around the floor kicking and screaming.

Angry

Stomped around the room knocking stuff off of shelves

Sat silently staring furiously into space.

Wept uncontrollably unable to catch her breath

Took several deep breaths, blowing his fury out with every puff

Glared at us with angry eyes sending chills down our backs

Paced back and forth like a nervous lion or crouched like a lion about to attack

The Story

It's a pleasant Friday afternoon, and you're feeling pretty good. Your homework is finished, your chores are done, and the whole weekend is yours. You're relaxing in your room, listening to the radio while playing your favorite video game. Just as you gobble up the last little creature, a voice comes over the radio, "Hey kids! How would you like to get a free yearly pass to <u>Disneyland</u>*? (Insert the name of a local amusement park.) Here's what you have to do. Just be one of the first twenty kids at our live broadcast at the McDonald's on Lee Street and Jordon Way tomorrow at 8:00 A.M."

Instantly your mind races. "That's the McDonald's down the street! I don't even need my parents to drive me there. Oh man, I can't believe my luck. I can get there before anyone!!" Checking with your parents for their okay, you make your plans. You'll get up at 6:00 A.M., get dressed, brush your teeth, eat breakfast, and be at the McDonald's by 7:00.

That night, you lay your clothes out on your dresser with your video game out on top just to give you something to do while you wait from 7:00 to 8:00 for the radio station to hand out the Disneyland* passes. With summer only one month away, you imagine yourself riding rides and stuffing your face with cotton candy every day from sun up to sun down. With a silly grin on your face, you go to sleep dreaming of roller coasters and parades.

Suddenly your eyes open, and the first thought to go through your mind is, "Wow, for 6:00 A.M., there sure is a lot of light coming in my bedroom window." In a flash, you're sitting straight up, realizing you forgot to set your alarm. "How could I be so stupid?" you shout as you jump out of bed. Looking at the clock, you see that it's 7:03. "I still have time if I skip breakfast and don't brush my teeth." Quickly, you reach for your clothes, but they're gone! You rush to your closet and there is NOTHING to wear! You reach under your bed for your dirty shorts with the chocolate milk stain all over it that you didn't want your mother to see. You put them on. To save time, you keep your Batman jammies shirt on and rush into the living room where all your clothes are in piles, ready to be washed. "Of all days to start spring cleaning!" Searching madly you can only find one shoe. "Mom, where's my other shoe?" you shout.

"I saw Skipper playing with it in the backyard. Maybe if you'd pick up after yourself, you'd find your stuff more quickly," she calls back, adding to your frustration.

You run into the back yard, and Skipper begins a playful game of keep-away. "I don't have time for this you bratty dog," you yell as Skipper begins a rousing game of tug-o-war with the shoe. "I'm going to tie your ears together, you crazy mutt, if you don't let go!" The dog lets go, and you fall back on your bottom right into a pile of dog mess.

Dirty, and now very smelly, you race out of the house with only forty-five minutes left. "I hope I'm not too late," you think as you imagine a long line of people already there waiting for their pass to Disneyland*. You run as fast as you can and in front of you, across the street, is the McDonald's with balloons, signs, and loud music blasting just for this special occasion. You race to make the light which starts flashing "Don't Walk", but you know you can still make it. Suddenly, two teenagers on bikes fly past you, knocking you down. They ride through the intersection into McDonald's and get in line while you get up and are stopped by the crossing guard. The anger starts to burn inside you as you begin to count the people in line in front of the radio station's colorful banner. One, two, three, four... all the way to eighteen. Oh man, there's still a chance. Come on light, turn green. "Turn green, turn green, turn green, turn green," you chant as you stare at the back of the guy who knocked you down praying that no one else gets in line ahead of you.

Finally, the light turns green, and you run faster than you've ever run before. You reach the back of the line to find one more person in the line, but that's okay. You are number twenty. Knowing this, a huge smile forms across your slimy, unbrushed teeth. You realize how ridiculous you look in your pajama top and dirty shorts, but you don't care. "I'm going to Disneyland*. I'm going to Disneyland*," you quietly chant to yourself. Yet, you won't let yourself really celebrate until you're holding the pass in your hands.

The glorious moment arrives. The radio announcer is telling his listeners about the contest and asks the kids in line to yell for his audience. He explains to the kids in line that when they get their passes, they should move behind the parking lot to get their pictures taken for the pass. So excited that you almost wet yourself, you count the people in front of you one more time. "Great, I AM number twenty," you tell yourself gleefully.

The first person gets her pass, then the second, and then the third. You can't help yourself. You're dancing from one foot to the other. Just another minute and the pass will be all yours. The tenth, eleventh, and twelfth people in line are given theirs. Your heart begins to pound, and your palms start to sweat. Only eight more left. The pimply-faced teenagers in front of you are blocking your view now, but that's all right. You're almost there.

Sixteenth! Seventeenth! Only the two teenagers ahead of you, and you're there. You can here the radio announcer talking to number seventeen, and your heart leaps knowing that, besides getting the pass to Disneyland*, you'll be on the radio too. "Wait until I tell all my friends. They'll be so jealous!" The first teenager is getting his yearly pass, and you're so excited you almost can't hold it in, when suddenly another teenager comes racing up on his bike. "Thanks, for saving my spot, dude!" he says as he high fives the guy in front of you. Before you can say anything, the radio announcer says, "... and these are the last two lucky winners of the year-long pass to Disneyland. What are your names fellas ..." The two teenagers begin talking to the DJ, and you're standing in shock. Didn't anyone see him cut in line? You turn to protest, but people are walking everywhere. "Hey, that guy cut in line!" you shout, but no one can hear. Your hopes and dreams have been stolen from you. No Disneyland*! No roller coasters! No cotton candy! No video games! Everything is gone, and there's NOTHING YOU CAN DO ABOUT IT!!!!!!!!!!!!!!

HOW DO YOU FEEL?
WRITE IT !!!!!!!!!

Beyond the Lesson

Put this on the board, and cluster the first paragraph with them. The rest is up to them:

(Free Passes
to Disneyland)

(I Woke Up
Too Late)

(Waiting In
Line)

Show-Not-Tell
Angry Paragraph
(Already Written)

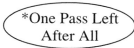
(*One Pass Left
After All)   * or create your
own ending.

Show-Not-Tell
Sad

After acting out the emotion, here is a cluster my students created.

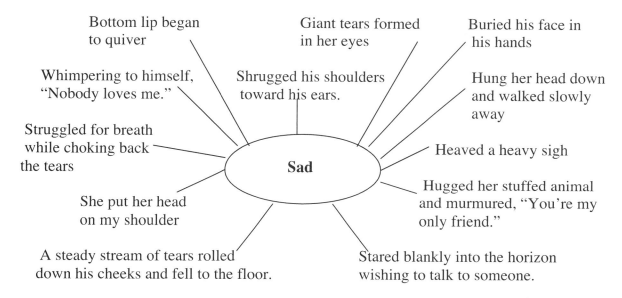

Bottom lip began to quiver

Whimpering to himself, "Nobody loves me."

Struggled for breath while choking back the tears

She put her head on my shoulder

A steady stream of tears rolled down his cheeks and fell to the floor.

Giant tears formed in her eyes

Shrugged his shoulders toward his ears.

Sad

Buried his face in his hands

Hung her head down and walked slowly away

Heaved a heavy sigh

Hugged her stuffed animal and murmured, "You're my only friend."

Stared blankly into the horizon wishing to talk to someone.

The Story

"King me!" you shout as the smell of victory is at hand. After several years and countless games of checkers, your best friend is finally going down. He's beaten you so many times, and now it is time for payback. Tap, tap, tap. After a swift double jump the game is yours. "Ha, a new champion is crowned. Thank you! Thank you," you call out to the imaginary audience as you wave, showing your appreciation.

"Enjoy it while it lasts," says Michael with a frown on his face that is unlike him. He is not a sore looser, so I know there is something else on his mind. It doesn't take long to figure out what it is. "I've got some bad news," he says. "My Dad got a new job. We're moving away next week." Moving away? What does that mean? Another block? Another city? Another state?

"Where are you going?" you ask, not really wanting to know the answer. Michael has been your best friend for as long as you can remember. You took swimming lessons together when you were six. You had the same teacher in first, second, and fourth grade. You had fought, laughed, and done the craziest stuff of your life together. Last Christmas Eve, you both took your bikes out in the rain and raced in the mud until you were both unrecognizable. Your mom made you hose yourselves off before letting you in the house.

"We're moving to Alabama," he says, his eyes gazing at the floor. You know what that means. You will probably never see him again. Both of you unable to speak, you just sit together fiddling with stuff until it's time to go home.

Every day that week you are over at Michael's house helping him and his family load a ton of stuff into boxes. You have a good time going through his old toys. Each one seems to have a special memory. There's the marble that you accidentally threw in the wrong direction. Boy, the knot it raised on his forehead was huge! You both laugh when he comes across the picture of him smashing the pie in your face during your eighth birthday party. You manage to have a good time with him despite the fact that you both know he is leaving for good.

The horrible moment comes when the moving van is packed and the family is ready to leave. Several people come to see them off. You have a hard time even looking at Michael. You feel that if you did, you'd start bawling right there in front of everyone. "Well, I guess this is it," he says.

"Yeah, I guess this is it." You reach out your hand, but he gives you a hug. Quickly he turns around and gets into the back seat of the car. As Michael and his parents wave good-bye, you watch the car slowly pull away. You stare into the back window of the car memorizing the moment. This is possibly the last time you will ever see your best friend. Just before they are out of sight, you see Michael turn around and wave one last time. Without a doubt, this is the saddest moment of your life.

HOW DO YOU FEEL?
WRITE IT !!!!!!!!!

Beyond the Lesson

Put this on the board, and cluster the first paragraph with them. The rest is up to them:

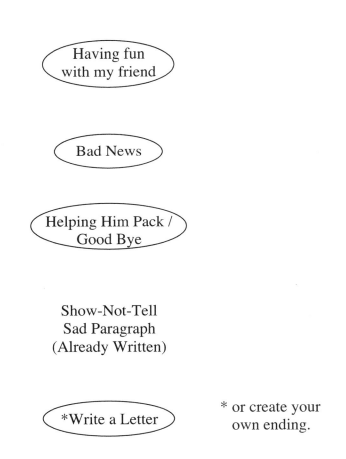

Show-Not-Tell
Setting

How to present these lessons:

A good time to teach these lessons is after teaching prepositions. Many prepositional phrases provide good support information about locations in a story and help involve the reader in the writing. (See Appendix for a complete list of prepositions.)   Some examples are:

... in the _____, ... toward the _____, ... around the _____,

...between the _____, ... above the _____, ... across _____.

These make good "mini-lessons" during writers' workshop, or you can teach this concept separately. Directions are included in the lessons. Once you've taught the concepts, require that your students use them in the next few assignments. If you don't do this, most of your students won't retain these skills.

Besides requiring that your students use the show-not-tell setting skills learned in the next few writing assignments, display a poster at the front of the class showing the show-not-tell skills they have learned. In this way, when you review the Writing Assessment Checklist, the students can see all of the skills they've learned, and they know that they have the tools they need to improve their scores.

Setting Introduction

I tell my students this story when I first teach a setting lesson and remind them of it whenever I teach other setting lessons. It helps remind them of the purpose for adding setting to their writing.

"What is the first image you see at the beginning of every episode of The Brady Bunch? They show a picture of the Brady house. Then they begin the story. Why do they do that? Because the show is really being recorded at a TV studio, and they want you to think that you are watching a real house and a real family. In television, this is called an "establishment shot." Every time the setting changes, they show you an establishment shot to make you feel like you are there. On Happy Days, when the guys are at the restaurant, Arnold's, they show you Arnold's before the action begins.

Good writers do the same thing. To show setting, sometimes we write a whole paragraph. Sometimes we only need a phrase. Involve your readers in the story by describing the setting. Let me show you how..."

Show-Not-Tell
Setting - Lesson #1
Posters

Lesson Overview: After reviewing Show-Not-Tell: Setting concepts, the students will write setting paragraphs inspired by popular movie posters that depict strong setting images.

1. Review the Writing Assessment Checklist. Emphasize that today's lesson will help improve #2, "Are their sentences show-not-tell sentences?"

2. Select a page from a book that you are reading as a class, and ask the students to point out words and phrases that show where or when something is happening. For example: A sentence in a book might say, "<u>Below the oak tree</u> which stretched <u>over Johnson's creek,</u> was a swarm of boys. <u>One by one</u> they swung <u>from the grassy bank</u> into the refreshing water."

   The underlined phrases point out settings that help visualize the story.

3. Give your students a copy of the prepositions from the Appendix. (I recommend that students keep this list in their writing folders for continual reference while writing.) Display a poster-sized copy of it in the classroom for students to use as a reference. Point out the underlined prepositional phrases in the example sentences in #2. Ask each student to select a preposition from the list and use it to describe an object in the room. Example: A picture of Mr. Dye's sons is <u>on his desk.</u>

4. Put two colorful posters on the wall. I used an <u>Aladdin</u> poster and a <u>Beauty and the Beast</u> poster. Give the students a few ideas on how to describe the settings of the posters. "Belle is dancing <u>in front</u> of the rose bush." "Iago is resting <u>on Jafar's shoulder.</u>"

5. Have the students on one side of the room write three sentences describing something on one poster, and the other half write three sentences describing something on the second poster. After sharing their ideas with the class, each half will repeat the activity with the other poster.

6. Have the students write a show-not-tell setting paragraph about one of the posters. Let the students select whichever poster they want.

Show-Not-Tell: Setting - Lesson #2
Magazine Pictures

Lesson Overview: Students will write Show-Not-Tell: Setting paragraphs using a picture from a magazine. The teacher will display the magazine pictures on the wall, distribute the setting paragraphs, and have the students match the paragraphs to the pictures on the wall.

1. Follow the review procedures from Setting – Lesson #1 to prepare the students for writing their setting paragraphs.

2. Bring in pictures from magazines (or have the students bring them) that have a great deal of activity. One student brought in a hotdog advertisement that showed a barbeque scene. A boy was diving into a pool while parents prepared to be splashed. A man in a chef's hat was putting hot dogs into buns, as a dog was chasing a cat through his legs, and Fourth of July decorations surrounded the back yard. This picture provided a wealth of ideas. Several students could write a paragraph describing this setting, and each paragraph would have a different point of view.

3. Select six pictures (8 to 10 pictures work well for larger classes). Divide the students into six groups. Give each group a picture. The students can brainstorm phrases that describe the pictures. After collecting fifteen to twenty ideas, the students write their paragraphs individually.

4. Collect the paragraphs. Be sure to keep each group's paragraphs together so you do not give a student a paragraph about his/her own picture. Distribute the paragraphs. Meanwhile, place the pictures on the wall. Label each picture A, B, C, etc.... Have the students write the letter of the picture on the paragraph that they think fits the picture.

5. Ask volunteers to read the paragraph that they were given. The students can tell which picture they felt matched the paragraph. As a class, discuss the strong points of the paragraph and generate ideas for making the paragraph stronger.

Show-Not-Tell: Setting - Lesson #3
Worksheets

The following pages contain two excellent worksheets to help students build their writing skills. The students simply collect setting phrases that are inspired by the pictures. The list of Show-Not-Tell Words at the end of this chapter would be a helpful resource for this assignment. Examples: **Hear**: crackling fire, symphony of crickets, crunch of rocks / **Smell**: pine scent, musty sleeping bag, fresh air / **Feel**: warmth of the fire, breeze in my hair, branches sharp points.

Complete the first paragraph as a class. Next, allow students to work in groups on paragraphs #2 and #3. Finally, have the students complete the rest of the paragraphs on their own. I found that these made excellent journal activities. The students should complete one each day until finished.

Directions:
1. List details that you might hear, smell, or feel in each picture.
2. Write a show-not-tell: setting paragraph about each picture below. Begin each paragraph by explaining <u>where</u> and <u>when</u> the scene is taking place.

Example: In the early evening as the sun is setting behind the trees deep in the Ozark mountains, a family prepares for their first night of camping.

1.

Hear: _____

_____

Smell: _____

_____

Feel: _____

_____

2.

Hear: _____

_____

Smell: _____

_____

Feel: _____

_____

3.

Hear: _____

_____

Smell: _____

_____

Feel: _____

_____

4.

Hear: _____

_____

_____

Smell: _____

_____

_____

Feel: _____

5.

Hear: _____

_____

Smell: _____

_____

Feel: _____

_____

6.

Hear: _____

_____

Smell: _____

_____

Feel: _____

_____

Extension: Select any setting paragraph from this worksheet. Write an entire story using the setting paragraph as the opening paragraph of your story.

Show-Not-Tell: Setting - Follow Up Ideas

1. Teaching the Where/When Writing Trick (See Ch.5) along with the setting makes this concept even more powerful. I require my fourth and fifth graders to begin every setting paragraph with this trick. Once the older students have mastered the skill, I allow them more independence.

2. Write a show-not-tell setting paragraph about this classroom. Do the pre-writing on the board as a class. I even write the paragraph on the board with them to help the students who still haven't caught on. Most students succeed after one or two attempts.

3. Write a show-not-tell setting paragraph about:

   (I don't assign these for homework until I feel the students have a firm grasp of this concept.)
   A. Your bedroom   B. The park   C. The playground   D. The library   E. A ballpark

4. Most writing assignments from now on should require that the students write something about the setting. Even research reports require some type of description of the setting. For example, my fifth graders wrote a report about the moon. I had them begin the report by describing what Neil Armstrong saw as he stepped onto the moon. There are so many ways to reinforce the concept of show-not-tell while learning new skills. Here are some examples of how to use show-not-tell to teach other skills:

Reading

Select descriptions of settings in student's reading books that employ good show-not-tell images. Have students make a list of the phrases used, write a summary of that section, then draw a picture of the scene - making sure that all the phrases they listed are included in the picture.

Example: In By The Great Horn Spoon, there is a chapter in which a cook chases a pig all around a boat. A boy who has adopted the pig is trying to save him. The writer paints eight great pictures with his words. I assigned groups of four to read one of these scenes, write about it, then draw the picture. The students were able to capture the imagery of the chapter, helping their reading comprehension. The class also had a great collection of pictures for our bulletin board as a reminder of the chapter. Finally, they added the list of show-not-tell phrases to their writing folder for future reference.

Social Studies

I ask students to research different places that we are studying, then write a show-not-tell paragraph describing it. For example, we took a field trip to Dana Point and toured the brig, Pilgrim. We used the vocabulary about ships and the items we saw on the boat to write our paragraphs. We also researched Williamsburg, colonial Boston, and Indian hunting grounds. Finally, we wrote paragraphs as if we were actually there.

This same strategy works well in science. For example, have your students research the blood stream, and pretend they are in a microscopic ship, sailing through the heart, lungs, and other areas of the body. A show-not-tell essay would be perfect for this.

Show-Not-Tell
Characterization

Show-Not-Tell: Characterization Introduction

Most states have reading standards that ask students to examine how characterization affects a story. There are writing standards as well that ask students to develop characters within their stories. With these worksheets, you will have a powerful tool to meet both of these standards.

The personality of a character greatly impacts the direction of a story. Many professional writers have stated that they develop their characters first and allow the personality of the characters to drive their stories.

After completing these worksheets, never again will your students write a story without thinking about the characters. By inventing the personalities of the characters ahead of time, your students will add depth to their stories that is very rare in pre-college writing.

Worksheets

The first worksheet (right) asks students to describe what certain personality types would do and say. This will help make them comfortable with the idea that writers have the power to create personalities by making the characters do and say things that influence a story.

The students will be given seven personality traits. They will then write a sentence that shows a character doing and saying something that fits that personality. By writing sentences, students will be less intimidated than if we ask them to develop characters within an entire story.

This second worksheet will begin to prepare students for actual story writing. First the students write sentences describing what different personality types would say and do. After they have collected this information, they will practice writing one paragraph stories that focus primarily on developing a character.

Follow Up

After your students have completed these worksheets, there are many activities that can develop this skill even further. Here is a list of activities to help your students improve character development in their stories:

1. Identify stories that have rich character development.

Begin by discussing famous movies that have larger than life characters. Disney films are famous for creating characters that have one dominant personality trait. Villains such as Captain Hook, Cruella DeVille, Maleficent, and the Evil Stepmother in Cinderella are classic examples of characters that are evil. The Seven Dwarfs in *Snow White* also provide opportunities to illustrate how personalities improve stories.

2. As a class, make a list of as many personality traits as you can. Write just one sentence showing an example of that trait. Mix up the Do's and Say's. This can serve as a reference.

   The poster (right) shows one my class created. It hung in our room for a couple of months. The students used it as a reminder and reference during writer's workshop.

3. The second worksheet asks the students to write one paragraph stories showing characters' personality traits. A good follow-up activity to this is to create mini-books. The students can select any four or five paragraphs to include in the book. Each page of the book focuses on a paragraph and its illustrations.

4. Have students write a story for which they create and develop several characters. It would be fun for students to create their own version of *Snow White and the Seven Dwarfs*. They can create four personalities (seven is too many for most students) and develop them within a story. The first year I did this project, "Samantha and the Four Weirdoes", many students said it was their favorite activity of the year.

> ## Characterization
> 1. **Flirtatious** – She stared deeply at him, batting her eyes and smacking her lips.
> 2. **Whimpy** – He began to whimper, crawled under the table, and covered his face as the mouse was let out of its cage.
> 3. **Maverick** – "You guys can go home if you want, but I'm going to catch that alligator," announced Wayne.
> 4. **Nerd** – Pushing her tapped glasses high on her nose, Devon warned the others, "You should buy a pocket protector like me."
> 5. **Serious** – While everyone laughed at the boy who fell, Charlie reached down and helped him up.
>
> **Personality Traits:** bully, whiner, cool, sweet, conceited, teacher's pet, cry-baby, joyful, sneaky, intelligent, stinky

What Is Characterization?

Every story has characters. However, not every story allows the reader to know what the characters are like. One terrific way to help your reader understand the story better is to give each character in your story a special personality.

How?

As you write your story, have your characters DO and SAY things that fit their personality traits.

Examples:

Personality: Whiner –

Do: Sarah folded her arms, lowered her head, and refused to speak to anyone.

Say: Sarah whined, "Why won't anyone play with me?"

Personality: Bully –

Do: Butch walked through the cafeteria grabbing chips off the plates of the first grade children.

Say: "Get out of my seat, punk!" ordered Butch as he pushed the girl off the bench.

Directions: Write sentences describing what someone with the following characteristics would Do and Say.

1. Nerd -

Do: _____

_____

Say: _____

_____

2. Cool -

Do: _____

_____

Say: _____

_____

3. Joker -

Do: _____

_____

Say: _____

_____

4. Sweet -

Do: _____

_____

Say: _____

_____

5. Bully -
Do: _____

_____

Say: _____

_____

6. Whiner -
Do: _____

_____

Say: _____

_____

7. Grumpy -
Do: _____

_____

Say: _____

_____

Extension: Make a list of five personality traits that would make a character interesting. On a separate sheet of paper, write a sentence explaining what someone with each characteristic would Do and Say.

1. _____

2. _____

3. _____

4. _____

5. _____

Part I – List two things a character with the personality traits below would Do and Say.

Example: Serious –

Say: It's time to quit fooling around and get back to work.

Do: Charles kept his nose in that book with his eyebrows crumpled in concentration for well over an hour.

A. Tattle-Tale

Say: 1. _____

_____

2. _____

_____

Do: 1. _____

_____

2. _____

_____

B. Know-It-All

Say: 1. _____

_____

2. _____

_____

Do: 1. _____

_____

2. _____

_____

Part II – Repeat the activity above on a separate sheet of paper for the following characteristics:

C. Teacher's Pet   D. Intelligent   E. Sneaky   F. Clumsy

Part III – Write a short story (one paragraph) for any three (3) characteristic above. Show a character in your story displaying that characteristic.

Show-Not-Tell
Poems

How to teach these lessons:

These poems will make good review for show-not-tell and can be taught by themselves or with a unit on poetry. In any case, a basic understanding of poetry is helpful before presenting these lessons. Be aware that these poems require a great deal of thinking. For the students who generally need extra help, you may want to present these in group settings.

Before Writing the Poems:

A. Read a few poems with your students.

B. Answer these questions with your students. Keep the answers on the board while they work:

What do you notice about poems? How are they different from paragraphs? *Possible answers:* Some poems rhyme, poems don't use complete sentences, etc...

C. Write a poem with your students to guide them in the process. The worksheet that the students will use is on the following page.

Here is a sample:

Poem #1

1. Emotion- <u>excited</u> - I high five all of my friends.

2. Why that
Emotion - <u>I hit a home-run</u> - A home run flys over the fence with one swing of my bat.

3. Emotion - <u>ecstatic</u> - I'm in the middle of a dog pile at home plate.

4. Setting - <u>The stands</u> - Parents cheering, opponents jeering, the fans are going crazy.

5. Three examples of
why you feel this - The game is ours! We won!
way.   This is so much fun.
The world thinks I'm second to none.

6. How you feel - <u>proud</u> - As though it had been chiseled on , a smile from ear to ear stretches across my face.

D. After editing for spelling and punctuation, have the students write and illustrate their final drafts. These make great bulletin board decorations.

I high five all of my friends after
A home run flies over the fence with one swing of my bat.
I'm in the middle of a dog-pile at home plate.
Parents cheering, opponents jeering, the fans are going crazy.
The game is ours! We won!
This is so much fun.
The world thinks I'm second to none.
As though it had been chiseled on,
A smile from ear to ear stretches across my face.

Show-Not-Tell
Poems

Poem #1 - This will be a poem about a time you experienced a strong emotion during an event in your life. Think of a time you felt very excited, sad, happy, angry, silly, or any other feeling. Write a word or phrase on the left, then think of a way to express it using show-not-tell.

Show-Not-Tell Phrase

1. Emotion- _____ ------- _____
   _____

2. Why that
   emotion?- _____ ------- _____
   _____

3. Emotion - _____ ------- _____
   _____

4. Setting - _____ ------ _____
   _____

5. Three examples
   of what made you   --------- 1. _____
   feel the emotion.   2. _____
                                        3. _____

6. How you
   felt - _____ ------ _____
   _____

Use your show-not-tell phrases to write your poem.

Poem #2 - This poem will be a story poem. Think of an event that would make a good story. Write a show-not-tell phrase for each part of the story.

Show-Not-Tell Phrase

1. Setting - _____

   _____

2. What is the

   mood? (Emotion) _____

   _____

3. Conflict (Problem) _____

   _____

4. What is the

   mood? (Emotion) _____

   _____

5. Rising Action _____

   _____

6. What is the

   mood? (Emotion) _____

   _____

7. Climax _____

   _____

8. What is the

   mood? (Emotion) _____

   _____

9. Resolution _____

   _____

10. What is the

    mood? (Emotion) _____

    _____

Use your show-not-tell phrases to write your poem.

Poem #3 - This poem will be about a place that is important to you. Use show-not-tell phrases to describe each area of this place. Next, explain how that place makes you feel.

Important Place: _____

Show-Not-Tell Phrase

1. Setting - _____ - _____

   _____

2. How this place

   makes you feel - _____

   _____

3. Setting - _____ - _____

   _____

4. How this place

   makes you feel - _____

   _____

5. Setting - _____ - _____

   _____

6. How this place

   makes you feel - _____

   _____

7. Setting - _____ - _____

   _____

8. How this place

   makes you feel - _____

   _____

Use your show-not-tell phrases to write your poem.

Show-Not-Tell Words

Directions: Keep these lists of show-not-tell words in your writing folder as a bank of descriptive words for your stories.

Sound Words

Loud Sounds: bang   bark   bawl   bedlam   blare   blatant   bluster   boom   brawl   bump   clamor   clap   clash   crash   deafening   discord   disorderly   earsplitting   explode   grate   hubbub   jangle   noise   pandemonium   piercing   racket   rage   rasp   raucous   riot   roar   rowdy   rumble   scream   screech   shout   slam   smash   squawk   stamp   stomp   thud   thunder   tumult   whine   whistle   yell

Soft Sounds: bleat   buzz   chime   clank   crackle   faint   gurgle   harmonious   hiss   hum   hush   inaudible   melody   murmur   musical   mute   mutter   patter   peep   resonant   rush   rustle   sigh   snap   speechless   still   swish   tinkle   twitter   whir   whisper   zing

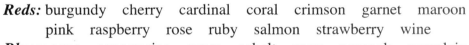

Speech Sounds: bellow   chatter   drawl   giggle   growl   guffaw   laugh   murmur   scream   screech   sing   snort   speak   stammer   stutter   talk   whimper   whisper   yell

Visual Words (Colors)

Reds: burgundy   cherry   cardinal   coral   crimson   garnet   maroon   pink   raspberry   rose   ruby   salmon   strawberry   wine

Blues: aqua   aquamarine   azure   cobalt   navy   peacock   porcelain   sapphire   sky   turquoise

Yellows: apricot   butter   buttercup   butterscotch   canary   gold   lemon   mustard   peach   persimmon   ochre   orange   sulfur   tangerine   topaz

Browns: almond   amber   beige   bronze   chocolate   cinnamon   coffee   copper   ginger   mahogany   nutmeg   rust   sandy   walnut

Greens: apple   celery   emerald   lime   mint   olive   pistachio

Purples: lavender   lilac   mauve   mulberry   orchid   plum   violet

Grays: ashen   dove   platinum   silver   steel

Whites: cream   ivory   oyster   marble   milky   pearl   snow

Blacks: charcoal   ebony   jet   licorice

Touch Words

cold   cool   crisp   damp   dry   dull   elastic   feathery   fleshy   fragile
furry   fuzzy   gritty   hairy   hot   icy   leathery   lukewarm   mushy   oily
pulpy   prickly   rough   rubbery   sandy   satiny   sharp   silky   slippery
smooth   soft   spongy   steamy   sticky   tender   tepid   thick   thin   tough
velvety   warm   waxy   wet   woolly

Smell And Taste Words

acrid   acidic   aromatic   bitter   bittersweet   bland   burnt   buttery
crisp   damp   dank   earthy   fishy   fragrant   fresh   fruity   gamy
gaseous   gingery   hearty   hot   mellow   mildew   moldy   musty
overripe   peppery   perfumed   piney   pungent   putrid   rancid   raw
reeking   ripe   rotten   salty   savory   sharp   sickly   sour   spicy
spoiled   stagnant   stench   sugary   sweet   tangy   tasteless   tempting
unripe   vinegary

"Said"

"Said" is such a boring word. Here is a list of substitutes.
Use them to paint a better picture.

A
accused
added
addresses
admitted
advised
announced
answered
apologized
argued
asked

B
babbled
badgered
bawled
beamed
begged
bellowed
blamed
blurted
boasted
bullied

C
cackled
cajoled
charged
chattered
chided
cited
claimed
coaxed
commanded
commented
complained
complemented
concluded
confided
confirmed
continued

contradicted
countered
cried

D
declared
decreed
demanded
denied
denounced
directed
disclosed
drawled
droned

E
elaborated
exaggerated
exclaimed

F
forecasted
fretted
fumed
fussed

G
gasped
gossiped
granted
greeted
growled
grumbled

H
hinted
howled

I
implied
implored
informed
inquired
insinuated
insisted
interjected
interrupted
introduced

J
joked
joshed
judged

K
kidded

L
lamented
lashed out
lectured
listed

M
maintained
mimicked
mocked
mumbled
murmured
muttered

N
nagged
narrated
negotiated
noted

O
objected
observed
offered
ordered

P
panted
pestered
pledged
pouted
proclaimed
promised
protested
puzzled

Q
quarreled
questioned
quoted

R
raved
recited
recalled
recollected
remarked
remembered
repeated
replies
reported
requested
responded
revealed
roared

S
schemed
scoffed
scolded
screamed

shouted
shrieked
sighed
snapped
snarled
sneered
sobbed
speculated
squawked
stammered
stated
stuttered
suggested

T
taunted
teased
testified
threatened
trembled

U
urged
uttered

V
vowed

W
wailed
warned
whimpered
whined
whispered

Y
yelled

Z
zinged

And Phrases

a lot

a lot of

because, cause, cuz

boring

etcetera (etc.)

glad

go (it goes, that goes)

good/bad

got

great

happy

I'm going to tell you about...

like

neat

nice

pretty

pretty good

really

so

so that

stupid

super

That's all.

The end.

This is about...

there

thing

you

you know

well

_____

_____

_____

_____

_____

_____

Chapter 4
Helping Students
Develop a Strong
Vocabulary

This chapter will:

1. Provide a variety of classroom tested techniques that help your students develop a strong vocabulary.

2. Guide you through some of the theory behind vocabulary development.

3. Help your students become life long learners of vocabulary by showing them simple, easy techniques to quickly learn new words.

Introduction

A strong vocabulary is critical to academic success, but vocabulary development takes a great deal of time and practice, and students tend to forget many of the words presented in each unit of study. For this reason, I included vocabulary in the Writing Assessment Checklist. It holds students accountable for using the words they learn in class. The lessons in this section foster retention and practical application of new vocabulary. They help students learn, retain, and employ new vocabulary when they write.

Vocabulary Lessons
and
Summaries

1. Picture Dictionary

The picture dictionary does several things. First, it helps students develop long term memory of their vocabulary words. Next, it creates a "bank" of words that they've studied, giving them a valuable collection of words that they can use in their writing. A great side effect of the picture dictionary is that it teaches an important study skill which can be applied to other areas of study. Finally, the picture dictionary does a great job helping students develop thinking skills. They are forced to give careful consideration to the definition in order to create the proper picture.

2. Power Vocabulary

I call this concept "Power Vocabulary" because it accomplishes several goals very effectively. Not only does this technique firmly plant definitions in the students' minds, it also provides powerful background information that helps prepare them for upcoming units of study. This front-loading strategy is a great way to begin any language arts, social studies, science, or any other unit of study.

3. Let Me Count the Ways

This lesson, which can be repeated as often as you like, helps build student vocabulary by giving students a variety of ways to say the same word. Knowing full well that the words we use help paint a picture, teaching this lesson is like giving students a set of different shades of the same color. A picture of the ocean would certainly be more realistic if the artist used several shades of blue rather than just one. In other words, this lesson helps the students use just the right word to describe exactly what they mean. For example, all students are familiar with the word "walk." We build around this word and add words like amble, stroll, march, saunter, and stride.

4. Paraphrasing

This is another lesson that forces students to carefully analyze, not only the meaning of the vocabulary word, but the meaning of the sentence as well. Combined with the picture dictionary or on its own, this is a powerful way to help students understand the meaning of difficult words in the context in which they are used.

5. Context Clues Worksheet

Most state language arts standards require the analysis of the text surrounding unknown words in order to determine their meaning. This worksheet will help your students learn to use context clues. Students record unknown words, infer their meaning based on context, verify accuracy using a dictionary and find synonyms. This technique works well with literature units, book reports, or read alouds

6. Student/Teacher

A vocabulary game that helps students review each other, peer tutor, and have fun learning vocabulary.

7. Sample schedule of a vocabulary unit.

Vocabulary
Picture Dictionary

About the picture dictionary:

Here is what the picture dictionary looks like. Use it with vocabulary units to help build retention. Punch holes in the margins so students can keep their finished work in their writing folders. They can use the picture dictionary while working on writing assignments, especially during the revising part of the writing process. This can be a very effective tool in your classroom. On vocabulary tests alone, 75% of my students receive A's. The ones who do not get A's are the ones who fail to do the picture dictionaries properly. For English learners, this is an especially effective tool.

Picture Dictionary (Continued)

How it works:

Whenever my students start a picture dictionary, they begin by writing two words at the top of the sheet: 1. Word and 2. Definition. This is to remind them of the two key steps. The first step is to draw a picture that sounds like or reminds them of the word. For example, if their vocabulary word is "dogma", they could draw a picture of a dog to represent dogma. Next, they think of how they can add something to that picture which represents the definition. In this case, "dogma" means "an established opinion or a strongly held position." To remember the definition, they can draw a picture of the dog saying, "In my opinion, I'm the cutest dog in the world."

This technique immediately puts the word and its definition into their short-term memory. The more they review the word, the more likely they are to retain it. When you begin a vocabulary unit, do four or five picture dictionaries with your students. After that, they are on their own. However, monitor their work carefully to make sure that they are doing it correctly.

After drawing the picture, it is crucial that the students explain why they drew what they did. Accept any picture as long as they can justify its content in the section to the right. They should state what they drew to represent the word and its definition. Example: dogma - "Dogma sounds like dog. Since dogma means 'an established opinion,' I made the dog state his opinion about himself."

Picture Dictionaries - Step By Step

Step 1 - Write the vocabulary word on the line.

Step 2 - Draw a picture in the box that represents:
1. The Word and 2. Definition.

Step 3 - Explain your picture in the space to the right.

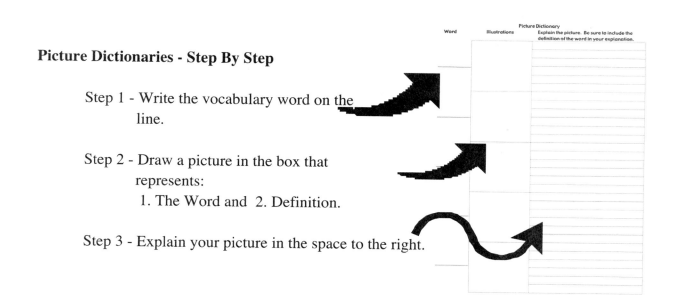

Picture Dictionary

Word	Illustration	Explain the picture. Be sure to include the definition of the word in your explanation.
_____		
_____		
_____		
_____		
_____		

Power Vocabulary

If you're looking for a way to teach vocabulary while introducing and reinforcing key language arts, social studies, and science concepts from your curriculum, you're in for a real treat with this lesson. While playing this "game", my students get to ask questions, and we have some of the best discussions of the year. My students enjoy our game, and, because they actively engage in learning, retain what they learn for the entire term.

Power Vocabulary
1) Find 10 strong vocabulary words.
2) Become an expert by writing the definition or a synonym of each word.
3) Make a Picture Dictionary for each word.

Teaching Your Words
1) Teacher says the words; students repeat. (2X')
2) Students say the words; teacher repeats. (2X')
3) Call out the #; students call the word (2X")
4) Call out a word; students say the # (2X')
5) Review your Picture Dictionaries with the group.
6) Call out a definition; students say the word. (2X')
7) Call out a word; students say the definition. (2X')

Procedure

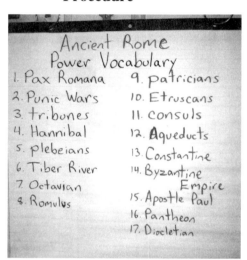

Ancient Rome Power Vocabulary
1. Pax Romana
2. Punic Wars
3. tribunes
4. Hannibal
5. plebeians
6. Tiber River
7. Octavian
8. Romulus
9. patricians
10. Etruscans
11. consuls
12. Aqueducts
13. Constantine
14. Byzantine Empire
15. Apostle Paul
16. Pantheon
17. Diocletian

Step 1 – Pronounce the Words

Make a list of twelve to fourteen words and number them. Post the list on the board or chart paper, and keep it on display as long as you are working on the unit. To make sure the students know how to pronounce the words, call them out and have the class say them after you. Repeat the procedure as needed. To the left is a sample list from one of our social studies units.

Step 2 – Students Lead

Reverse the procedure. Having the class call out the words for you to repeat gives students the opportunity to practice without your help. Your repeating each word confirms its correct pronunciation. Help them stay together as they pronounce the words by pointing to the class when it is their turn.

Step 3 – Word Game

Studies show that students must hear a word over thirty-six times in order for it to enter their short-term memory. At this point, students have been engaged with the list of new words only a few minutes, yet they have heard the new words several times and are already becoming familiar with them.

This game will enhance your students' recognition and understanding of each new word. Call out a word and have the class tell you which number matches it. The fun begins when students try to call out the numbers faster than their neighbors. Mix up the game by having only the girls respond and then the boys. Have those in the front half of the class try it; then those in back.

Step 4 – Number Game

Play the game in Step 3, but reverse roles. You call out a number, and have the students call out the corresponding word.

Learning the Definitions

Suggestions:

Flashcards – Ask students to write the word on one side of a card and the definition on the other. They can then use the cards to quiz a partner.

Worksheets – Many of your language arts series have vocabulary worksheets. Use those or you can make your own.

Vocabulary Review – Review the vocabulary words as you do the Power Vocabulary activity. If you do this activity with ten to twelve words, the students pick up on the definitions quickly. Make sure you give the students a list of the definitions, or post them somewhere in the room. If this is how you are reviewing the definitions, just move on to Step 5.

Step 5 – Definition Game A

Call out a definition. Have the class tell you which word matches it, and follow the same procedures as in Steps 3 and 4.

Step 6 – Definition Game B

Repeat Step 5, but reverse roles. You call out a word, and have the students call out the corresponding definition.

Follow Up

Power Vocabulary is effective because it's fun, there is a lot of repetition, and it moves very quickly. You can spend as much, or as little, time on it as you want. Here are some other ideas on how to use this activity.

1. Introduction Activity – I use Power Vocabulary at the beginning of every social studies and science unit as a front loading activity. It is a great way to introduce the unit. They will be seeing so many of these vocabulary words throughout the unit, it is a good idea to give the students a good head start with this game.

2. Review Activity – When I do this activity with my literature units I will spend the first five minutes of each lesson reviewing the vocabulary. If it takes us three days to read a story then they've had many opportunities to internalize the words.

3. Spelling Unit – Sometimes, your new vocabulary words make a great spelling unit. Begin by giving the words as a pretest. Complete the Power Vocabulary routine and have students write each word in a sentence for homework. You may want to give a combination vocabulary/spelling test. After you have called out the spelling words, call out a definition and have your students write the letter "A" next to the corresponding word, a "B" next to the word corresponding to the second definition you call out and so on.

Student Lead Power Vocabulary

Students can create their own Power Vocabulary game using the Power Vocabulary and Definitions double-sided worksheet on the following pages. Let them choose the words and run the game. They can select words from book report books, literature circles, chapters from a book you are reading as a class, or social studies/science chapters. The directions follow.

Power Vocabulary   Name: _____

1. _____   6. _____

2. _____   7. _____

3. _____   8. _____

4. _____   9. _____

5. _____   10. _____

Student-led Power Vocabulary

In this activity, students select ten words from a text chosen by the teacher and take turns leading a group of three or four classmates in the Power Vocabulary game.

1. Students select ten words from their literature book and write them on the front of the worksheet (above right). They should print the words large enough for everyone in their group to see. It might help if they use a crayon or marker.

2. Students look up the definitions and write them on the back of the worksheet (left).

3. The students take turns leading their group in the game. The purpose of this activity is for the leader to practice pronouncing the words for the group to repeat. Next, the students can play the game calling out numbers and words. Finally, they can share the definitions.

Power Vocabulary

1. _____

2. _____

3. _____

4. _____

5. _____

6. _____

7. _____

8. _____

9. _____

10. _____

Definitions

1. _____

_____

_____

_____

2. _____

_____

_____

_____

3. _____

_____

_____

_____

4. _____

_____

_____

_____

5. _____

_____

_____

6. _____

_____

_____

_____

7. _____

_____

_____

_____

8. _____

_____

_____

_____

9. _____

_____

_____

_____

10. _____

_____

_____

Vocabulary
Let Me Count the Ways

About this lesson:

This lesson was designed to help students find a variety of ways to say common words. Because the words we choose help to paint a picture, the ability to chose precisely the exact word we mean is a tremendous asset. This lesson teaches students how to "count the ways" they can say the same word.

Words like walk, smart, big, laugh, steal, clever, and weird are very common but do not always convey the same meaning in every situation. For example, a nervous person might pace rather than walk. Someone who is bored might amble, wander or stroll.

If students write a common word on the front of an index card and five of its synonyms on the back each week, by the end of the year the students will have a list of two hundred words to use in their writing. Also, the index cards make great flash cards for vocabulary review.

This is a good assignment to do as a class, individually, or to do as homework. It also works well as an assignment when you have a substitute teacher.

How it works:

Step 1 – Give each student a copy of the Let Me Count the Ways worksheet. As a class, select a common word that can be said in a variety of ways. Give the students a list of words, and let them choose or select a word of your own. (Model the process on the board, overhead, or chart paper.) Write the word on the top line. See the underlined words above for examples.

Step 2 - Have the students look up the word in the thesaurus and make a list of five of its synonyms on the board. Go over the synonyms and explain how each is different. For example: "giggle" is different than "snicker." Giggle is a nice, playful laugh and snicker is a laugh that makes fun of others. The students can decide, with your guidance, which five synonyms they would most likely use in their writing.

Step 3 - Use the five new words to fill in the worksheet. Write them on the numbered places below the common word. The students can use the dictionary to find the definitions of each synonym. If the dictionary gives a sample sentence showing how the word is used, it can be entered in the "sample sentence" space. If not, help them think of a sentence that illustrates the word.

Note: There is a sample lesson on the following pages followed by a test. Steps 1-3 have been done for you. If you wish, you can use these five common words. Have your students save their flash cards each week and use them to study for this cumulative test.

Step 4 - Draw a picture dictionary type picture (see previous section) in the box to help remember the definition of the word.

Step 5 - Give each student six index cards. On the first card, have them write the common word on the front and five synonyms on the back. On the other five cards, they write the new word (synonym) on the front and its definition on the back.

** After doing this lesson a few times, you can test the students on the words they've learned.

Review of Steps #3-5 of the Let Me Count the Ways worksheet

Step 3 - Write the common word here:

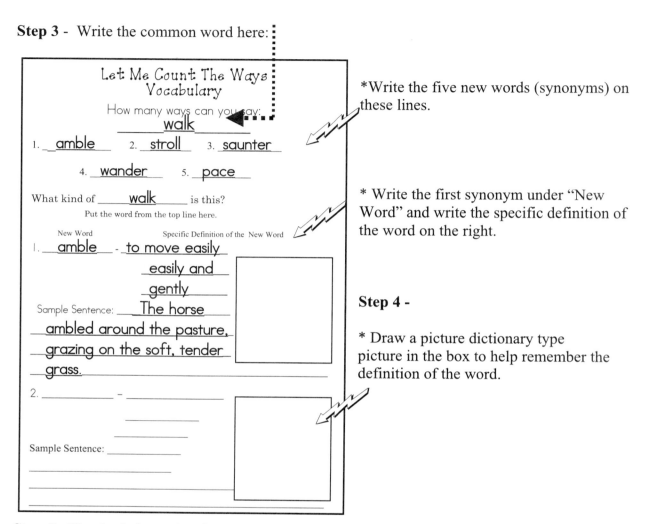

Let Me Count The Ways Vocabulary

How many ways can you say:

_____walk_____

1. _amble_   2. _stroll_   3. _saunter_

4. _wander_   5. _pace_

What kind of ___walk___ is this?

Put the word from the top line here.

New Word   Specific Definition of the New Word

1. _amble_ - to move easily

_____easily and_____

_____gently_____

Sample Sentence: ___The horse_

ambled around the pasture,

grazing on the soft, tender

grass.

2. _____ - _____

_____

_____

Sample Sentence: _____

_____

_____

*Write the five new words (synonyms) on these lines.

* Write the first synonym under "New Word" and write the specific definition of the word on the right.

Step 4 -

* Draw a picture dictionary type picture in the box to help remember the definition of the word.

Step 5 - Use the information from the worksheet to make flash cards. The flash cards can be used to study for their test. The worksheet can be used as a reference for their writing.

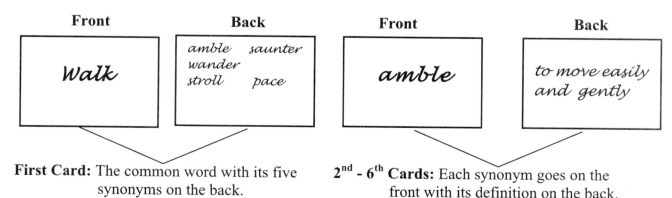

Front	Back	Front	Back
Walk	amble saunter wander stroll pace	*amble*	*to move easily and gently*

First Card: The common word with its five synonyms on the back.

2ⁿᵈ - 6ᵗʰ Cards: Each synonym goes on the front with its definition on the back.

Let Me Count The Ways
Vocabulary
How many ways can you say:

Name: _____

_____

1. _____ 2. _____ 3. _____

4. _____ 5. _____

What kind of _____ is this?

Put the word from the top line here.

New Word   Specific Definition of the New Word

1. _____ - _____

_____

_____

Sample Sentence: _____

_____

_____

_____

_____

2. _____ - _____

_____

_____

Sample Sentence: _____

_____

_____

_____

_____

3. _____ - _____

_____

_____

Sample Sentence: _____

_____

_____

_____

_____

4. _____ - _____

_____

_____

Sample Sentence: _____

_____

_____

_____

_____

5. _____ - _____

_____

_____

Sample Sentence: _____

_____

_____

_____

_____

Let Me Count the Ways

Said
1. whispered – A quiet form of said.
2. protested – The way you say something when you <u>don't agree</u>.
3. expressed – The way you say something when you're sharing an idea.
4. uttered – To briefly say something.
5. harangued – To give a long, long persuasive speech or lecture.

Crazy
1. delirious – Acting crazy because of an illness or hallucination.
2. demented – Criminally insane behavior.
3. imbecilic – Idiotic kind of crazy.
4. insane – Medically crazy.
5. maniacal – An evil kind of crazy.

Afraid
1. cowardly – Afraid like a coward.
2. aghast – Being shocked.
3. timid – A shy kind of afraid.
4. terrified – Afraid for your life.
5. faint-hearted – Slightly afraid; Afraid to the point of being uncomfortable.

Laugh
1. chuckle – A good healthy laugh.
2. cackle – A laugh that sounds like a hen laying an egg.
3. snicker – A quiet, mean laugh because of someone's misfortune.
4. giggle – A fun, playful laughter.
5. jeer – Laughing at someone to make fun of them.

Smart
1. adroit – Skillful, clever, and smart in different circumstances.
2. apt – Quick to understand; Very capable.
3. witty – Smart humor; Cleverly humorous.
4. ingenious – Smart creativity; Being able to invent.
5. dexterous – Smart in hand-eye coordination.

<u>Test</u>

Let Me Count the Ways
Test

_____ 1. whispered A. Idiotic kind of crazy.

_____ 2. delirious   B. A shy kind of afraid.

_____ 3. cackle   C. Smart humor; Cleverly humorous.

_____ 4. chuckle   D. A quiet, mean laugh because of someone's misfortune.

_____ 5. witty   E. A good healthy laugh.

_____ 6. expressed F. Skillful, clever, and smart in different circumstances.

_____ 7. maniacal   G. An evil kind of crazy.

_____ 8. aghast   H. A quiet form of said.

_____ 9. jeer   I. Smart in hand-eye coordination.

_____ 10. apt   J. To briefly say something.

_____ 11. harangued K. The way you say something when you're sharing an idea.

_____ 12. imbecilic   L. Criminally insane behavior.

_____ 13. timid   M. To give a long, long speech.

_____ 14. giggle   N. Acting crazy because of an illness or hallucination.

_____ 15. adroit   O. Being shocked.

_____ 16. dexterous   P. A fun, playful laughter.

_____ 17. snicker   Q. A laugh that sounds like a hen laying an egg.

_____ 18. protested R. Laughing at someone to make fun of them.

_____ 19. uttered   S. The way you say something when you don't agree.

_____ 20. demented T. Quick to understand; Very capable.

Vocabulary
Paraphrasing

About Paraphrasing:

In this lesson, the students are required to <u>find the vocabulary words</u> from sentences in their reading books and <u>rewrite the sentence in their own words</u>. This requires some advance preparation on your part as you must identify the pages on which the words are found. Paraphrasing forces the students to think about the definitions of the words. Also, it helps their reading comprehension because they have a head start on the more difficult sentences in the book. Below is a sample of a unit my students completed and some of the sentences they wrote.

Sign of the Beaver
Vocabulary
Chapter 1-7

(Pg.3) 1. daub - to smear or pat a substance on something.
(Pg.5) 2. rueful - feeling sorry for a wrong doing.
(Pg.9) 3. proprietor - the owner of a store.
(Pg.9) 4. treaty - a written agreement between two nations.
(Pg.9) 5. horrid - intensely disgusting.
(Pg.9) 6. gravely - wrong, very serious.
(Pg.10) 7. startle - to scare because of a quick surprise.
(Pg.10) 8. quavering - to shake or tremble.
(Pg.10) 9. loon - a fish eating, diving bird
(Pg.10) 10. mournful - full of sadness.
(Pg.10) 11. boughs - a branch on a tree.
(Pg.13) 12. passel - a large number.
(Pg.14) 13. drawl - to speak in a slow, dragged out tone.
(Pg.16) 14. fierce - eager to kill or injure; ferocious.
(Pg.17) 15. begrudging - unwilling to give up or do
           something.

The Vocabulary Unit

You can collect the words as a class from the book they are reading, or the students can collect their own. The unit shown here takes a great deal of time to develop and is not necessarily needed for this assignment. Find the words any way you want. The objective of this lesson is to have the students rewrite the sentences in their own words.

Examples:

Sentence from the book:
1. "<u>Ruefully</u>, he trudged back to the cabin."

Student paraphrased sentence:
1. "<u>Upset at himself</u>, he walked back home."

Sentence from the book:
2. "Since the last <u>treaty</u> with the tribes, there had not been an attack reported anywhere in this part of Maine."

Student paraphrased sentence:
2. "Since the last <u>agreement</u> made with the Indians, they had not attacked anyone in Maine."

Sentence from the book:
3. "The two men had nodded to each other <u>gravely</u>"

Student paraphrased sentence:
3. "The two men looked at each other <u>very seriously</u>."

Vocabulary
Paraphrasing

Part 1 - Directions:

As you read, find *ten (10)* words whose definitions you *do not know*. Write the words on the lines below. Be sure to write the page numbers where you found the words on the small lines to the right. (Unless, of course, you like hunting through the book for words.)

1. _____ ____

2. _____ ____

3. _____ ____

4. _____ ____

5. _____ ____

6. _____ ____

7. _____ ____

8. _____ ____

9. _____ ____

10. _____ ____

Part 2 - Directions:

Look up the above words write their definitions on the lines below.

1. _____

_____

2. _____

_____

3. _____

_____

4. _____

_____

5. _____

_____

6. _____

_____

7. _____

_____

8. _____

_____

9. _____

_____

10. _____

_____

Part 3 - Directions:

On a separate sheet of paper, rewrite the sentences from the book in your own words.

Vocabulary
Context Clues

Directions:

1. Find vocabulary words from the story you are reading. Write the words and page numbers on the lines below.
2. Context: Read the sentence from the story and, based on the context, try to figure out what the word means. Next to "My Guess", write what YOU THINK is the definition of the word.
3. Real Definition: Look up the word in the dictionary. There may be more than one definition. Write the definition of the word that matches how the word is used in the sentence.
4. Write a synonym for the word.

1. _____ - _____ : My guess (definition) - _____

   Real Definition: _____

   Synonym: _____

2. _____ - _____ : My guess (definition) - _____

   Real Definition: _____

   Synonym: _____

3. _____ - _____ : My guess (definition) - _____

   Real Definition: _____

   Synonym: _____

4. _____ - _____ : My guess (definition) - _____

   Real Definition: _____

   Synonym: _____

5. _____ - _____ : My guess (definition) - _____

   Real Definition: _____

   Synonym: _____

6. _____ - _____ : My guess (definition) - _____

   Real Definition: _____

   Synonym: _____

7. _____ - _____ : My guess (definition) - _____

   Real Definition: _____

   Synonym: _____

8. _____ - _____ : My guess (definition) - _____

   Real Definition: _____

   Synonym: _____

Vocabulary
Student / Teacher

How it works:

      This is a great review game that works for spelling as well as vocabulary. A great time to play this game is a day or two before a test.

    Step 1 - Have the students label their paper like the example below. Label the column on the left "Vocabulary Words" (or "Spelling" words if you are using this as a spelling review game.) Label middle column "3 Times Each" and the right column "Points."

    Step 2 - Have the students work in pairs and decide which student will be the "Student" and which student will be the "Teacher."

    Step 3 - The "Teacher" will look at the vocabulary list with the definitions and read the definition of any word on the list. The "Student" will write the word that fits that definition in the left column. (For the spelling review, the "Teacher" will say the spelling word and the "Student" will spell it.)

    Step 4 - The "Teacher" will draw a happy face in the middle column if the "Student" answers correctly and write "2" in the points column on the right. If the answer is incorrect, the "student" must write the correct word three times in the middle section, and receives "0" points.

** I find that 7 minutes for each student is plenty of time before the game begins to get boring. After 7 minutes, I call out, "Switch! Student becomes teacher, teacher becomes student."

Vocabulary Words	Three Times Each	Points
1. 2. 3. 4. 5. 6.		

Sample Schedule of a Vocabulary Unit
Using the Picture Dictionary

Day 1

Hand out the vocabulary list, and complete the Power Vocabulary activity. Do the paraphrasing assignment, context clue assignment, or start picture dictionary.

Day 2

Do a picture dictionary for two of the vocabulary words as a class. Students do three on their own.

Day 3-5

Repeat the Day 2 activity until all the vocabulary words have been completed. As the students work, walk around the room and quiz them on the pictures they've already finished. I give raffle tickets to students who can explain the pictures they drew AND define the words we've covered on previous days.

Day 6

Play Student/Teacher with the vocabulary words as a practice test.

Day 7

Play a vocabulary review game.

Day 8

Vocabulary Test

Chapter 5
Writing Tricks That Add Style
to Your Students' Writing

This chapter will:

1. Show you how to teach your students to write in a variety of intelligent styles.

2. Provide worksheets that will help your students master over a dozen writing techniques.

3. Help you create a system to help your students master writing skills and apply them in all writing situations.

4. Reinforces grammar skills by applying grammar rules within the context of writing.

What are Writing Tricks?

Writing tricks are specific writing skills that help the author communicate more intelligently. There are thousands of techniques writers use to communicate more effectively. By giving these techniques a name, your students can now identify specific ways to improve the quality of their sentences.

Here are a few examples of writing tricks:

* With a terrier in hot pursuit, the cat ran up the tree, through the branches, and onto the roof. - **Prepositional Phrase**
* What would you do if you won the lottery? - **Attention Getter**
* My dad whispered in my ear, "Son, I've never been prouder." - **Dialogue**

Why Writing Tricks?

I wanted a system that would not only teach my students writing skills, but would allow them to apply the skills in their everyday writing and retain them for a lifetime. Giving the skill a name enables the students to identify it and use it on a regular basis. Before creating this program, I was leery of teaching grammar rules such as appositives because I felt that only a handful of students would retain the skill. By treating it as a writing trick and naming it "Appositives," my students learned to identify the appositive as a specific way to improve their writing. They also retained the rules of grammar that apply to it.

I keep a list of the writing tricks I've taught during the year at the front of the classroom for my students to use as a reference while they work on writing assignments. Also, while we read stories together in class, the students are quick to point out the writing tricks used in the book. Because the writing tricks and the Writing Assessment Checklist are posted in the class, my students regularly identify good writing skills when they see them. Therefore, the writing trick system trains students recognize great writing, which will surely help them become better writers.

About this section:

This section helps you teach dozens of specific skills your students will use for a lifetime. It will also help them recognize effective writing when they see it because they will have a way of categorizing the sentences that they know create better writing. There are enough writing tricks here to keep you busy for a couple of years. I've never been able to teach more than twelve in one year, but you may find time for more. For home-schooling parents, you may eventually run out, but I encourage you to start creating writing tricks of your own.

Teaching the Writing Tricks:

This chapter contains dozens of worksheets I've created over the years. Some were designed specifically for third graders, and some for seventh graders. Therefore, review the worksheets carefully before giving them to your students. You can easily modify many of the worksheets to match the grade level of your students.

Another important thing to consider is that many of the worksheets are meant to be used AFTER background information is taught. For example, before teaching the adjectives writing trick, I teach a short unit on adjectives. My students have no problem with the worksheet because they already know about adjectives. You will be the best judge of how much background information your students will need before each worksheet is assigned.

In any case, here is a sample lesson plan on how I help these writing tricks become an integral part of my students writing:

Step 1 - Teach any background knowledge needed for the writing trick. (Example: Before assigning the worksheet on prepositions, teach the students the definition of a preposition and have them write a few prepositional phrases of their own.

Step 2 - Teach the worksheet. Check for understanding. If several students don't grasp the skill, stop, review the skill, and try again. (I've had to do this from time to time. With persistence, most of my students do just fine.)

Step 3 - Follow up the worksheets by giving assignments that require students to use the trick in their writing. Do this several times until class understands the skill. Here are a few ideas:

Journal Writing: Example - Use the writing trick "adjectives" to write five sentences about different people you know.

Homework: Example - Write a paragraph about a pet you or a friend owns. Use the writing trick "adjectives" at least 2 times. Use any two other writing tricks we've learned at least once. Skip lines and underline the tricks.

Class Writing Assignment: Example - Write an essay about a character in the book we are reading. Be sure to use the writing trick "adjectives" at least three times, and use any three other writing tricks at least once. Skip lines and underline the writing tricks.

Here is an example of a practice assignment:

<u>"There's a snake in my bed!"</u> screamed Sarah as she began pounding furiously on
(Attention Getter and Dialogue)

her sleeping bag. <u>My heart pounding</u>, I raced into her tent <u>like a bolt of lighting</u>. There was
(Introductory Phrase)   (Simile/Metaphor)

hissing coming from somewhere, so I grabbed Sarah's <u>skinny, trembling arm</u> and pulled her
(Adjectives)

outside the tent. By now Mom, Dad, and my two brothers surrounded the space where the serpent
(Lists)

lurked, each carrying a weapon to pound its evil head. <u>"On the count of three be ready to strike!"</u>
(Dialogue)

yelled my father <u>like a general going to war.</u> On "three" the sleeping bag came up, and we all
(Simile/Metaphor)

pounded that snake with all our might. When the dust settled, we were all embarrassed to find

that we had just killed my sister's <u>leaky air mattress</u>.
(Adjectives)

     I can't begin to tell you how exciting it is to see students write like this when just a few months before, they were barely writing complete sentences. I enjoy watching their faces as I make a big deal about their writing assignments. They know I'm telling the truth about how much they've improved because they can compare their current work to writing samples from the beginning of the year. Because they've learned to use the Writing Assessment Checklist, they recognize effective writing techniques when they see them, especially in their own writing. This builds a tremendous amount of confidence which is important for young writers.

Comma Rules
as
Writing Tricks

1. Dialogue

2. Introductory Phrase / Introductory Clause

3. Appositives

4. Interrupter

5. Direct Address

6. Words in a series

7. Phrases in a series

Hints for Teaching
"Dialogue"

Before using the worksheet:

 * Read stories rich in dialogue. While reading, ask the students to point out what makes sentences with dialogue different from other kinds of sentences. Guide them to these ideas:

- The exact words spoken by a character are enclosed in quotation marks.
- The quotation is treated as its own sentence. For example, the first letter is capitalized, it ends in a punctuation, and it follows the rules of sentence writing.
- Have students explain the difference between dialogue and paraphrasing.
- Point out what dialogue looks like at the beginning of a sentence, and what it looks like at the end of a sentence.
- Can you find dialogue that is split in the middle of the sentence?
- Can you find dialogue that contains several sentences in the same quote?
- When do they indent and begin new paragraphs because of dialogue? When there is a new speaker, the dialogue will be indented.

Beyond the Worksheet:

 Create as many opportunities for the students to use dialogue as possible. Here are some suggestions:

- Homework: Write a paragraph about something you did this week. Use the dialogue writing trick three times.
- Write a story about your family. Include quotations from at least three members of your family.
- Write paragraphs about people you are studying in other subjects. Include quotations from these characters used.

 Over the next few weeks, whenever your students write, always require that they use dialogue. Older students can begin practicing indenting whenever a new character speaks.

Writing Tricks
Dialogue

Three Ways to Write Dialogue:

    1. "Clean your room, or no dessert for you," said Mom.

    2. "Clean your room," said Mom, "or no dessert for you."

    3. Mom said, "Clean your room or no dessert for you."

Directions:

    Re-write the following sentences so they include writing tricks. Write each sentence two (2) times, using two (2) different styles.

1. Dad told me to rake the leaves.

    A. _____

_____

    B. _____

_____

2. Pat asked me to go to the movies.

    A. _____

_____

    B. _____

_____

3. I yelled for the zoo keeper to watch out for that big, ugly gorilla about to grab him.

    A. _____

_____

    B. _____

_____

4. Jeff asked the teacher how long it was until lunch.

    A. _____

_____

    B. _____

_____

5. The vampire told the maiden that he wanted to suck her blood.

    A. _____

_____

    B. _____

_____

6. The little girl told her daddy that she loved him.

    A. _____

_____

    B. _____

_____

7. The students pleaded for Mr. Dye to give them an "A" on their test.

    A. _____

_____

    B. _____

_____

8. On a separate sheet of paper, write a story about a friend who doesn't want to do the same thing you want to do. Use at least five (5) dialogue exchanges within your story.

Hints for Teaching
"Introductory Phrase/Clause"

Before Using the Worksheet:

* Teach the definition of a phrase and clause. Have your students repeat after you:

    "Word; Phrase: a group of words; Clause: a group of words which contains a subject and a predicate; Sentence: a group of words which contains a subject and a predicate, and expresses a complete thought."

    You can extend this to **"Paragraph: a group of sentences about one main idea; Essay: a collection of paragraphs on one theme."** You will have several opportunities to review this skill as you teach other writing tricks in this book.

* During your reading time, identify sentences with introductory phrases. Copy down words that are used to begin these phrases, and discuss what additional information the introductory phrase gives to the sentence.

* Ask your students to observe the following: Are all introductory phrases followed by a comma? (For the purposes of our worksheet, I ask the students to always use a comma after the introductory phrase, but it is not always needed.)

* Use the lists of subordinating conjunctions and prepositional phrases to practice writing phrases.

Beyond the Worksheet:

Introductory phrases/clauses offer students the opportunity to share information about when something is taking place. Therefore, have the students write about events that have several aspects to them. Here are some examples:

- **Homework:** Write a paragraph about what happened at school today.

- **Review:** Have students review lessons taught in other subjects, such as history or science, by writing sentences about the lessons using this writing trick.

- **Journal:** Write an introductory phrase or clause on the board. Have the students write five different ways to finish the sentence. The next day, do the reverse. Write a sentence on the board, and have the students write five introductory phrases or clauses.

- **Play a Game:** Have student A write a phrase or clause. Student B finishes the sentence. Repeat as time allows.

Writing Tricks
Introductory Phrase

Prepositions

about	above	across	after	against	along
amid	among	around	at	before	behind
below	beneath	beside	between	beyond	but
by	despite	down	during	except	for
from	in	inside	into	like	near
of	off	on	onto	out	outside
over	past	since	through	throughout	to
toward	under	underneath	until	up	upon
with	within	without			

Directions:

Use the list of prepositions to write sentences with introductory phrases about the topics below. Write your answers on a separate sheet of paper.

Example:
A storm: _During the storm, we took shelter inside a cave._

1. A fire:

2. School:

3. Lunch:

4. Camping:

5. A video arcade:

6. The eye of a hurricane:

7. The movies

8. An assembly:

9. A mountain:

10. A pack of wild dogs: 11. The ocean: 12. The rain forest:

13. An amusement park: 14. The Grand Canyon: 15. A space station:

Writing Tricks
Introductory Clause

Directions:
Use the list of subordinating conjunctions to write sentences with introductory clauses on the following topics.

Example:
A Storm: _Before the storm arrived,_ _we placed sandbags along the road_ _to keep the floods away from our_ _house._

Subordinating Conjunctions		
after	once	unless
although	since	until
as	so	when
as if	than	whenever
because	that	where
before	though	wherever
for	till	whether
if		while

1. The Park:

2. River Rafting:

3. Vacation:

4. A Concert:

5. Television:

6. A Restaurant:

7. An Amusement Park:

8. A Roller Coaster:

9. Cotton Candy

10. The Ocean:

11. The Beach:

12. A Zoo:

13. The Desert

14. Rock Climbing

15. A Pie Eating Contest

Hints for Teaching
"Appositives"

Before Using the Worksheet:

* Teach the definition of an appositive. Have my students memorize: "An appositive is a noun or pronoun that explains, identifies or renames the noun or pronoun next to it." Next, the students give me an example such as: Mr. Dye, my writing teacher, taught us how to write appositives. / or / My writing teacher, Mr. Dye, taught us how to write appositives.

* Point out appositives when you are reading with your students. Discuss reasons why this is such an effective writing technique. Point out these possible reasons and others that come to mind.

- They clarify possible confusing parts of your writing for the reader who may not be familiar with an item or person.
- They give additional information without breaking the flow of the story or essay.

Beyond the Worksheet:

Create as many opportunities as possible for the students to use appositives. Here are some suggestions:

- Homework: Write a paragraph about a place you know very well. Use the appositive writing trick three times to describe the people and items.
- Write a story about a birthday party. Use appositives to describe the guests, the presents, and the decorations.
- Write paragraphs about people and objects you are studying in other subjects. Use appositives to describe people and objects that are relevant to those topics. For example: Photosynthesis, the process through which plants turn light into food, would make an interesting topic for my science project.

Writing Tricks
Appositives

Directions: Read the sentences below and combine them into one sentence using appositives. Write your sentences on a separate sheet of paper.

Example:

Mr. Dye wants me to practice my writing tricks to improve my writing skills. He is my fifth grade teacher.

Mr. Dye, my fifth grade teacher, wants me to practice my writing tricks to improve my writing skills.

** Remember, there may be more than one way to write the sentence.

1. Gretel is my miniature schnauzer. She will do tricks for food.

2. My friends and I went on Space Mountain six times. It is the best ride in the park.

3. Minutemen were soldiers who were ready to fight on a moment's notice. They fought the British army at the Battle of Lexington.

4. Honolulu is one of the most popular cities in the world. It is the capital of Hawaii.

5. When we get to Big Bear we're going to race down the slopes. It is the best place for skiing.

6. Be sure to study isosceles triangles because there will be several questions about them on the test. An isosceles triangle has two equal sides.

7. Thomas Jefferson was the third president of the United States. He sent Lewis and Clark out to explore the Louisiana Purchase.

8. Tommy said, "Angelica needs our help to make lemonade." Tommy is Chucky's cousin.

9. Mr. Smith is the best coach in the league. He's won five baseball championships.

10. We're going to the Grand Canyon for summer vacation. Summer vacation is only two weeks away.

11. Steven was equivocal about his involvement in the fight at recess. Equivocal means not completely truthful.

12. Our principal was very explicit about his punishment. Explicit means very clear.

13. Randall will challenge Roxanna to a game of handball at recess. Randall is the best handball player at the school. Roxanna is the second best handball player at the school.

14. Francis Drake was an English pirate. He sailed around the world plundering Spanish ships.

15. I enjoyed listening to <u>The Four Seasons</u> while doing my homework. <u>The Four Seasons</u> was written by Antonio Vivaldi.

Extension:

You are a tour guide for your school. Create a guide book for your school describing the people (teachers, students, administrators), clubs, important areas, and special events of your school. Use at least seven appositives in your book.

Hints for Teaching
"Interrupter"

An "interrupter" interrupts the normal flow of a sentence. The interrupter is set apart from the rest of the sentence by being placed between commas. A comma will begin and end the interruption.

For example: Bunting, a skill in baseball that takes years to master, is an important technique that can mean the difference between winning and losing.

An interrupter gives the reader crucial information about a subject when it's not convenient to go into detail about that particular piece of information. In the example sentence, it is important to realize that bunting is not an easy skill to master. I used the interrupter to convey that point and then went on with my sentence.

Similes and metaphors make great interrupters. When students begin to write their own interrupters, similes and metaphors help them get off to a good start. Example: Rounding third, running as quick as lighting, the player tripped over the base and slid head first into the dirt.

Before Using the Worksheet:

This worksheet works well when taught with "Appositives." It is basically the same idea, and the students generally understand the interrupter easily after learning the appositive. I strongly recommend finding several interrupters within your literature books. Some authors use them more freely than others. Once the students are skilled at locating interrupters in literature, writing them is much easier.

Beyond the Worksheets

Create as many opportunities as possible for students to use interrupters. Here are some suggestions:
- Homework: Write a paragraph about an activity you did this week. Use the "interrupters" writing trick three times.
- Write a story about your family. Include interrupters that tell interesting facts about them.
- Write paragraphs about people you are studying in other subjects. Interrupt the flow of the sentences by telling something about the person that is related to the main idea of the sentence. Example: George Washington, having had a great deal of military experience in the French and Indian War, was the obvious choice to become the head of the Continental Army.

Writing Tricks
Interrupter #1

What is an interrupter? An interrupter interrupts the normal flow of thought in a sentence. The interrupter should be placed between commas.

	Interrupter
* The problem, I guess, will never be solved.	, I guess,
* Many players, like Johnny, had struck out against this incredible pitcher.	, like Johnny,

Directions: Put commas before and after the interrupters in the following sentences. Pay attention to the interrupters. You will be writing sentences like these when finished.

1. The playground of course needs a new set of equipment before school starts.

2. The season starts my dad told me in three weeks.

3. If we don't get back from our vacation however I won't be able to make it.

4. Janice having had the best grades all year had the best chance to receive a scholarship.

5. This paper for example has no name on it and will therefore receive an "F".

6. The students who study on the other hand will do very well on the test.

7. The dozens of players chosen for the All-Star team including many of the players on our team will be going to Cooperstown this summer.

8. Molly Pitcher after a hard day of helping the American soldiers finally joined in the battle herself when her husband collapsed on the field.

9. David's walk home after having fallen into the lake was terribly uncomfortable because of his soaking wet clothes.

10. The lunch room cleared when Mike who was known for his powerful sneezes began to reach for a tissue.

Writing Tricks
Interrupter #2

Directions: Write a sentence using the word or phrase in parentheses ( ) as an interrupter.

Example: (trying to be helpful) <u>The boy, trying to be helpful, held the nails but knocked over the paint.</u>

1. (waiting for the bus) _____
_____
_____

2. (for example) _____
_____
_____

3. (however) _____
_____
_____

4. (including everyone in our class) _____
_____
_____

5. (who likes to play practical jokes) _____
_____
_____

6. (in my opinion) _____
_____
_____

7. (buzzing around like bees to honey) _____
_____
_____

** Write a one paragraph story based on any three of the sentences above.

Hints for Teaching
"Direct Address"

In direct address, the writer simply states the name of the person or group to whom someone is speaking. It may not be very flashy, but it's a good way to emphasize a point. When used with dialogue, it has even more of an impact. In many cases, stating the name of the person or group being addressed adds drama to the story. At the beginning or end of a sentence, the direct address is set apart by a comma. In the middle of a sentence, it is surrounded by commas just like an interrupter. Here are three examples:

Men, today we go to war!

Today, men, we go to war!

Today we go to war, men!

Before Using the Worksheet:

One way to introduce this writing trick is to select two students and make a request of each one. **First**, pick a student toward the back of the class and say, "Please bring me your pencil." Normally, the student will say, "Who, me?" Next, ask another student, "Kim, please bring me your pencil." This student will normally do what you ask. Now, ask the class to tell you how the two requests about the pencils differed. The main points to get across are: Saying the name of the person got the student's attention, there was less confusion, and it helped you get what you wanted more quickly. **Next**, write the three sentences about war (from above) on the board, and reemphasize the main points using the sentences as examples.

After this introduction, ask the students why there are not quotation marks around these sentences. Some students confuse direct address with "dialogue." No one is quoted in direct address. Rather, someone is spoken to by another. To illustrate this point, write: *The general announced*, in front of one of the sentences. Now the students can see the difference: The general announced, "Men, today we are going to war!"

Beyond the Worksheet:
- <u>Writing Assignments</u>: After the students finish the worksheet, have them write a paragraph in which they use this writing trick at least three times. Assign topics that will foster the use of this type of writing trick. Examples: Write about a project you completed with friends; Make up a story about an emergency and make yourself the hero; or Write about a fun family experience.
- <u>Journal</u>: Write five sentences using the direct address writing trick. Topic: What a teacher would say at an assembly.
- <u>Homework</u>: Write five direct address sentences using real sentences said to you by other people. Invent the direct address if no one said anything directly to you.

Writing Tricks
Direct Address

Direct Address refers to the use of a name or personal pronoun to identify the person to whom someone is speaking. Direct Address is set apart with commas when it interrupts the sentences. At the beginning or end of a sentence, it is set apart with a comma. Here are three examples:

Emily, you may have some cookies if you help me bake them.

You may have some cookies, Emily, if you help me bake them.

You may have some cookies if you help me bake them, Emily.

Directions: Rewrite the sentences below three different ways using a direct address at the beginning, middle, and end just as in the examples above.

1. We're going to the movies tomorrow if you would like to come.

_____

_____

_____

2. If you keep scratching that mosquito bite, it won't heal.

_____

_____

_____

3. What you give is what you get.

_____

_____

_____

4. Do you know how important you are to me?

_____

_____

_____

5. The funny thing about today is that I was there too.

_____

_____

_____

6. It's your turn to do the dishes, not mine.

_____

_____

_____

7. You aren't supposed to go swimming right after you eat!

_____

_____

_____

8. When you turn in your homework, put your name on it.

_____

_____

_____

9. What do you think will happen if I push that button?

_____

_____

_____

10. The hotdogs taste good, but the hamburgers taste funny.

_____

_____

_____

Hints for Teaching
Words in a Series / Phrases in a Series

The danger of this writing trick is that some students use this technique to tell their entire story in one sentence. A student may write an entire story about what happened on a camping trip in a sentence or two using "Phrases in a Series." The purpose of this trick is to evoke specific visual imagery about a specific event. It also increases the pace of a story when used with verbs, a technique which is very effective in scenes involving a lot of action. When used with prepositions, it increases the imagery of the setting.

Before Using the Worksheet:

Months before I teach this writing trick, I prepare my students by calling attention to words and phrases in a series while we read aloud in class. I refer to them as "lists." I even offer raffle tickets to students who point them out. Over the weeks, I'll ask what the word "series" means, and why they think the author chose to use this writing trick rather than another. By the time I'm ready to teach this trick, the students are prepared to learn it and typically do so very quickly.

Beyond the Worksheet:

Explain that when using words or phrases in a series, the words or phrases must follow the same pattern within the list. Otherwise, once your students begin using this trick in their writing, you may begin to notice a common error.

For example: The <u>tall, blond, golfing</u> man made his putt. This is not grammatically correct because "tall" and "blond" are adjectives and "golfing" is a verb used as an adjective. All of the words must be the same part of speech.

Second example: The cat <u>raced up the tree, across the fence, and jumped onto the mouse</u>. This is also incorrect. The first and third items in the list begin with verbs. Notice how "across the fence" does not start with a verb. This error can be corrected by adding a verb at the beginning of the second phrase such as "ran across the fence." Now all of the phrases are the same. The error can also be corrected by deleting the verb "jumped." Now all of the phrases are prepositional phrases.

These are very common errors and are to be expected. They indicate that your students are grasping the concept of this writing trick and have the courage to risk making mistakes when they write. Take advantage of the opportunity to correct these mistakes when they occur. Most students who attempt this trick in their writing typically catch on fairly quickly so continue to give assignments that require them to use this trick.

Writing Trick
Words in a Series

Definition

When you list several words in a sentence, it is called "Words in a Series." The words may be nouns, adjectives, verbs, or adverbs. Be sure to place a comma between every item in the series. See the examples below.

Examples:

Nouns: While cleaning under the couch, we found <u>crumbs, coins, and toys.</u>

Adjectives: The sunset filled the sky with an array of <u>orange, yellow, blue, and red</u> tones.

Verbs: We <u>packed, changed, and ran</u> out the door.

Adverbs: The ants managed to find their way <u>on to, between, and underneath</u> our picnic blankets. **(Also)** We <u>slowly, carefully, and nervously</u> carried the wet painting into the sun to dry.

Directions: Write two (2) sentences about each picture. Use "Words in a Series" in each sentence. Be sure to use different parts of speech for each picture.

1. _____
   _____
   _____
2. _____
   _____
   _____

1. _____
   _____
   _____
2. _____
   _____
   _____

1. _____
   _____
   _____
2. _____
   _____
   _____

1. _____
   _____
   _____
2. _____
   _____
   _____

1. _____
   _____
   _____
2. _____
   _____
   _____

1. _____
   _____
   _____
2. _____
   _____
   _____

1. _____
   _____
   _____
2. _____
   _____
   _____

1. _____
   _____
   _____
2. _____
   _____
   _____

Writing Trick
Phrases in a Series
Definition

When you list several phrases in a sentence, it is called "Phrases in a Series." They can be noun, adjective, verb, preposition or adverb phrases. Be sure to place a comma between every phrase in the series. See the examples below.

Examples:

Nouns: <u>Men and women, boys and girls, and children of all ages,</u> come see the greatest show on earth!

Verbs: The cat <u>raced up the tree, zoomed across the fence, and pounced on the large ball of yarn.</u>

Adjectives: At our slumber party, there were <u>silly kids pillow fighting, noisy girls gossiping, and tired parents hiding.</u>

Prepositions: The ball bounced <u>into the street, against the curb, and onto the porch.</u>

Adverbs: The arms of the ride went <u>in and out, up and down, and back and forth.</u>

Directions: Use the topics below to write sentences using "Phrases in a Series." Be sure to use each part of speech from above at least once.

Describe the contents of your pocket.	1. _____ _____ _____
Describe what you did at a carnival.	2. _____ _____ _____
Describe what you need for a party.	3. _____ _____ _____
Describe how a cat ran through a yard.	4. _____ _____ _____

Describe a plane flying through the air.	5. _____
Describe what you do when you meet a movie star.	6. _____
Describe what bees are doing around a hive.	7. _____
Describe what you did on a camping trip.	8. _____
Describe the items in a trick-or-treat bag.	9. _____
Describe what an area looks like after a tornado.	10. _____
Describe what you feel while standing on the beach.	11. _____
Describe what you see at a circus.	12. _____

Parts of Speech
as
Writing Tricks

1. Adjectives

2. Vaunting Verbs

3. Ly-How Adverbs

4. Prepositional Phrases

Hints for Teaching Adjectives

This common writing trick will help struggling and average writers become better writers in a short amount of time. It's fun, easy to learn, and easy to identify while reading. There is no shortage of examples when trying to find sentences to use as models for your students.

I begin teaching this writing trick on the first day of school, and I've noticed an interesting side effect. As with many of the writing tricks, my students begin using it when they speak. Therefore, I encourage them to incorporate writing tricks in their speeches when they present oral reports which makes their speeches much more interesting. The wonderful surprise that I've found is the number of the students who use these techniques in our everyday discussions. So, not only are they learning to write intelligently, they are learning to speak more intelligently as well.

Before Using the Worksheet:

You can choose to teach a large or small unit on nouns and adjectives. All this lesson needs to accomplish is that the students acquire a basic understanding that adjectives describe people, places, or things. To warm the students up for this worksheet, you might point around the room and have them use this writing trick to describe objects that they see. For example,

"a large, decorative bulletin board; long, black hair; bright, shining lights; glossy, new books; clear, sunny day; etc..."

During these warm-ups, pick topics that will allow students to practice this trick using all of their senses. You can choose foods to describe how things taste, a fishing trip to describe how things feel, an amusement park to describe how things sound, and a candy store to describe the smells.

Be sure to explain that for this writing trick, the two or three adjectives you choose should not be synonyms. "The big, gigantic elephant" would not be correct because "big" and "gigantic" have the same meaning. You will see this type of mistake several times when they first begin using this trick. When someone makes this mistake, write the sentence on the board and have the class try to figure out why the sentence is incorrect. The students will catch on pretty quickly.

Beyond the Worksheet:

Create as many opportunities as possible for your students to use the adjective writing trick. Here are some suggestions:

- Homework: Write a paragraph about a day at the beach. Use the adjective writing trick three times. Use it to describe how something looks, feels, and smells. (You might want to pre-write ideas for sights, textures and smells at a beach with the younger students.)
- Write a story about people in your class. Use adjectives that describe their looks, personality, and anything about them that you like. Be sure to use ONLY positive or friendly descriptions.
- Write sentences about people you are studying in other subjects. Use adjectives to describe them. Example: The cold, determined soldiers at Valley Forge suffered for an entire winter during the American Revolution.

Writing Tricks
Adjectives

Definition: Placing 2 or 3 adjectives are placed in front of a noun counts as a writing trick.

Example: The <u>boy</u> with the <u>voice</u> asked the <u>teacher</u> a question.

The <u>small, handsome boy</u> with the <u>high, squeaky voice</u> asked the teacher a question.

Instructions: Use the Adjectives Writing Trick to change the sentences below. You can add adjectives to one or all underlined nouns.

1. The <u>man</u> had a <u>mole</u> under his right eye.

_____

_____

2. My <u>sister</u> spilled <u>juice</u> on my <u>shirt.</u>

_____

_____

_____

3. The <u>athlete</u> slammed the ball into the <u>basket.</u>

_____

_____

4. A dog was in our <u>garbage</u> ripping the <u>trash</u> into <u>pieces.</u>

_____

_____

5. The <u>sky</u> was filled with <u>clouds.</u>

_____

_____

6. With her trunk, the elephant grabbed the peanut.

_____

_____

_____

7. There's a monster under my bed!

_____

_____

_____

8. Her eyes were as shiny as the sun.

_____

_____

9. The fire engine raced past the kids.

_____

_____

_____

10. Four people fell into the pool at my party.

_____

_____

_____

_____

Hints for Teaching Vaunting verbs

This writing trick could have been called "exciting verbs," but I felt it would be a good experience for the students to learn a good vocabulary word, so I used "Vaunting Verbs." "Vaunting" means bragging. Explain to your students that Vaunting Verbs brag about themselves. They are better than common, often overused verbs. The use of common verbs such as said, hit, and walk would result in boring sentences while the use of vaunting verbs such as utter, pummel, and amble produce sentences that paint a much better picture and deserve to be called vaunting verbs.

The goal of this writing trick is to help students use a variety of vocabulary words. The richer their vocabulary, the more descriptive their writing. The Let Me Count the Ways vocabulary program expands this writing trick into weekly vocabulary drills that help students improve their writing as they enrich their vocabulary.

Before Using the Worksheet:

This worksheet will ensure that students have a basic understanding that verbs are action words. Once your students are comfortable identifying and recalling their own action words, they are ready to begin this writing trick.

Try having your students find verbs in their literature books, and discuss whether they are boring verbs or vaunting verbs. When students begin making judgments about the quality of words in others' writing, they begin to be more selective of the words they use. This is an effective way to motivate them to expand their vocabulary, and it gives them a sense of pride to know that their writing has improved because of the words they've chosen.

Beyond the worksheet:

- Homework: Use the vaunting verbs from your worksheet in a story.
- Have your students circle the verbs in their writing that they think are common. Give them the blank worksheet, and have them create their own list of vaunting verbs. The fact that this list comes from their own vocabulary gives it more significance and makes this a powerful learning tool.

Writing Tricks
Vaunting Verbs
1

Directions:

Think of at least four vaunting verbs to replace each of the following common verbs.

said   ran

jumped   hit

look   walk

laugh   think

Fill in each empty circle with a common verb. Next, write 4 vaunting verbs around each circle.

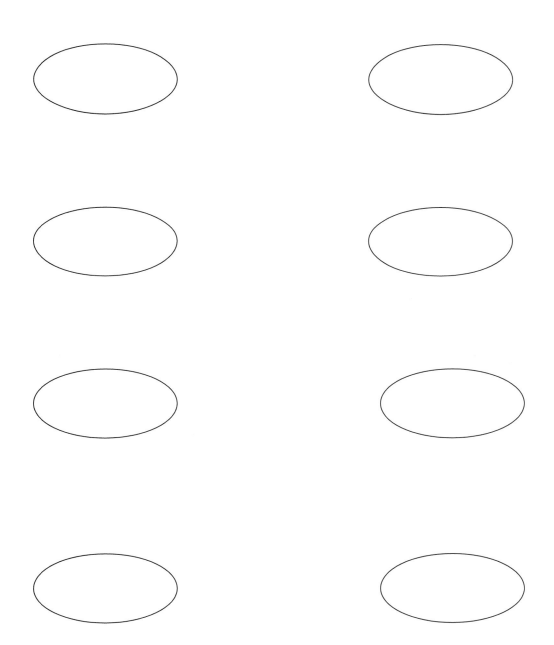

Writing Tricks
Vaunting Verbs
2

Replace each common verb below with two vaunting verbs.
Next, write two sentences using each vaunting verb.

1. said   __begged__   _suggested_
   __Shelly begged her dad for a gold fish._____
   __Shelly's dad suggested, "How about a gold fish._____

2. ran   _____ _____
   _____
   _____

3. jumped   _____ _____
   _____
   _____

4. hit   _____ _____
   _____
   _____

5. look   _____ _____
   _____
   _____

6. walk   _____ _____
   _____
   _____

7. laugh   _____ _____
   _____
   _____

8. think   _____ _____
   _____
   _____

Hints for Teaching
"Ly-How Adverbs"

This writing trick is called "Ly-How Adverbs" for several reasons. First, it reinforces the idea in your students' minds that adverbs answer the question "How?" Adverbs that end in "-ly" typically do this. The second reason for this title is to distinguish the Ly-How adverb from other kinds of adverbs. The "-ly" adverbs paint a very specific picture in the mind of the reader. The third reason for the title is that my students enjoy raising their hands and saying, "How," like an Indian when we talk about this writing trick. While not entirely politically correct, it aids long-term retention of this concept.

Before Using the Worksheet:

I recommend teaching a unit on adverbs before you introduce these worksheets. At the very least, review the function of adverbs. Another good idea is to point out Ly-How adverbs in the students' literature, and ask how the sentences would be different without the adverb. When the students themselves explain why sentences are better with the adverbs, they are far more likely to use them.

Beyond the Worksheet:

- Save samples of your students' work. Have them use a crayon to highlight verbs in each other's writing, and then write a Ly-How adverb above each verb.
- Journal: Write five Ly-How adverbs on the board. Have the students write one sentence using each adverb.
- Homework: Write a story about an activity at recess. Use at least five Ly-How adverbs in your story.

Writing Tricks
"Ly-How Adverbs"
#1

Directions: Change the following adjectives into adverbs by adding "-ly". For the words with a * , you will need to change the spelling of the word when adding "-ly".

1. quiet = _____

2. cautious = _____

3. careful = _____

4. safe = _____

*5. happy = _____

6. brave = _____

7. quick = _____

8. neat = _____

9. stubborn = _____

10. nervous = _____

*11. crazy = _____

12. ignorant = _____

13. ridiculous = _____

14. beautiful = _____

*15. noisy = _____

16. soft = _____

17. sad = _____

18. sarcastic = _____

*19. angry = _____

*20. gentle = _____

Writing Tricks
Ly-How Adverbs
#2

Directions: Rewrite each of the sentences below by adding an adverb that ends in -*ly*. Remember, the Ly-How Adverbs describe <u>how</u> the verb was done. The verbs have been underlined for you.

Example: The baby <u>crawled</u> across the floor.
The baby <u>crawled</u> *quickly* across the floor.

1. We <u>walked</u> through the house so we would not wake anyone.

_____

_____

2. The waitress <u>carried</u> the hot soup across the crowded restaurant.

_____

_____

3. The glass dish was <u>wrapped</u> and <u>placed</u> in the box for shipping.

_____

_____

4. After the boat sank, everyone was able <u>to swim</u> to shore.

_____

_____

5. Shawn <u>crossed</u> the stage to receive his award for most valuable player.

_____

_____

6. Seeing the girl in trouble, Peter <u>fought</u> the dogs away with a stick.

_____

_____

7. With only ten minutes before school started, Kristlyn <u>grabbed</u> her books and <u>ran</u> out the door.

_____

_____

8. The wrestler <u>swung</u> his victim around the ring.

_____

_____

9. This being her very first flight, Ashley <u>boarded</u> the airplane.

_____

_____

10. Carlos <u>jumped</u> around the field because the umpire called him out.

_____

_____

11. "We're going to be late if we don't hurry," Dad <u>yelled</u>.

_____

_____

12. Wishing she owned one, Jennifer <u>eyed</u> Jessica's Rug-Rats poster.

_____

_____

Writing Tricks
Ly-How Adverbs
#3

Directions: Rewrite each of the sentences below by adding an adverb
that ends in _ly_. Remember, the Ly How Adverbs describe how
the verb was done. The verbs have been underlined for you.

Example: The baby <u>crawled</u> across the floor.
The baby <u>crawled</u> _quickly_ across the floor.

1. Selena <u>walked</u> into the boys' bathroom thinking it was a classroom.

_____

_____

2. The students <u>laughed</u> for ten minutes because they won a bet with their teacher.

_____

_____

3. Jessica <u>sang</u> in front of the school.

_____

_____

4. The students <u>entered</u> the cafeteria.

_____

_____

5. My mother <u>kissed</u> my forehead and said, "Pleasant dreams."

_____

_____

6. "Herman, my goldfish, is dead," said Liliana.

_____

_____

7. "That was smart," Joseph said after I spilled my juice.

_____

_____

8. The woman marched out of the meeting because she lost the election.

_____

_____

9. The puppy sniffed the box, wondering if there was a treat for him inside.

_____

_____

10. "I'm not eating those pickles" David said.

_____

_____

11. My heart beat as the roller coaster raced down the hill.

_____

_____

Follow Up: Use each adverb from worksheet #1 in a sentence.

Ex. Having won the award for best speller, Roxanna smiled contently for the camera.

Hints for Teaching
Prepositional Phrase

Using prepositional phrases is a wonderful way for students to add descriptive details to a story. The details they add are typically ones they would not have considered had they not been using this trick. Once students have become familiar with this trick, they begin to use descriptive phrases with ease. To qualify as a writing trick, I require my students use at least two prepositional phrases in the sentence.

Before Using the Worksheet:

Explain the definition of a phrase (a group of words). Give the students a list of prepositions, and have them write their own phrases. Each day, warm-up the class by having each student think of a prepositional phrase, and have them share it with the class. Once they are comfortable thinking of prepositional phrases, they are ready to write sentences that contain them.

Be sure to point out prepositional phrases in books. Ask the students to explain why these sentences are better than those without prepositional phrases. In most cases, prepositional phrases make the setting of a situation more descriptive. For example: *The man _with the black briefcase_ handcuffed _to his wrist_ dashed _into the limousine_ which raced _around the corner_.* The setting in this sentence is enhanced because we can see what the man is carrying (black briefcase), where it is (on his wrist), where he went (into the limousine), and where it went (around the corner).

Once this writing trick is mastered, the elementary writer has graduated to a new level of writing.

Beyond the Worksheet:

- Have the students trade writing papers and add prepositional phrases to each other's writing. Also, during the revision phase of their writing, have them add prepositional phrases to their own writing.

- Keep a preposition poster on the wall for the students to use as a reference while writing.

- Homework: Write sentences using prepositional phrases. Use topics that require many details about a setting such as: a park, a trip to the beach, visiting the zoo, a birthday party, etc...

Writing Trick
Prepositional Phrase
#1

Directions:

1. Write a prepositional phrase for each preposition.

2. Write a story using each preposition once. Remember, the preposition must be used in a phrase. If not used in a phrase, it is an adverb.

Writing Trick
Prepositional Phrase
#1

Directions:

1. Write a prepositional phrase for each preposition.

2. Write a story using each preposition once. Remember, the preposition must be used in a phrase. If not used in a phrase, it is an adverb.

Writing Trick
Prepositional Phrase
#2

Directions: Rewrite the sentences using <u>at least</u> two prepositional phrases.
The "X" indicates a good place to add a prepositional phrase.

              X   X

Ex. The bird sang a beautiful song .

The bird <u>in the tree</u> sang a beautiful song <u>at the top</u> <u>of its lungs</u>.

    X   X X

1. A boy watched the skateboarders race.

_____

_____

  X   X   X

2. I go to my grandmother's house every Thanksgiving.

_____

_____

       X   X

3. Monica's cat sprinted.

_____

_____

  X   X X

4. The dinner bell rings.

_____

_____

  X   X   X   X

5. Santa Claus travels   to give all the good boys and girls their presents.

_____

_____

     X   X   X

6. The girl met the eyes of a boy.

_____

_____

No more X's will be given. You're on your own.

7. A deer nibbled on some fresh, green leaves.

_____

_____

8. The man blew his nose fifty times.

_____

_____

9. I like to eat hamburgers.

_____

_____

10. The roller coaster races quickly.

_____

_____

11. We went to Chuck-E-Cheese.

_____

_____

12. A burglar waited to rob the store.

_____

_____

13. The judge warned the criminal.

_____

_____

14. Cookies are the best treats.

_____

_____

Poetry Terms and More
as
Writing Tricks

1. Simile/Metaphor

2. Hyperbole

3. Idioms

4. Personification

5. Onomatopoeia

6. Where/When

Hints for Teaching
"Simile / Metaphor"

Simile	Metaphor
Comparing two things using "like" or "as"	Comparing two things using "is" "are" "was" "were" and "am". * Is, Are, Was, Were, and Am do not need to be present. Example: We keep marching in this parade called life. = Life <u>is</u> a parade.

I've taught the simile/metaphor writing trick every year I've been teaching, and it has always been popular with my students. They notice them very quickly when we read together in class, and they enjoy putting all kinds of them in their writing. The use of a simile/metaphor is a quick and easy way to spice up any piece of writing.

Before Using the Worksheets:

Ask the students to answer these questions:

How soft is a pillow?

How hungry would you be if you hadn't eaten all day?

How fast is (pick a popular athlete)?

Explain that sometimes the best way to describe something is to use similes and metaphors. Go through the questions again and answer them with similes and metaphors. Then have the students make up their own.

Beyond the Worksheets:

– <u>Writing Assignment:</u> Write a paragraph describing someone in the class using similes and metaphors. (Be nice!) Don't say the name of the person. Pass the paragraphs around, and have students try to guess the name of the person being described in each paragraph. (This is fun and provides students an opportunity to see several examples of similes and metaphors.)

– <u>Homework:</u> Describe a stormy day using five similes or metaphors.

– <u>Journal:</u> Describe how you feel today using similes and metaphors.

– <u>Reading:</u> Have students point out similes and metaphors when they see them in literature. It reinforces the concept and highlights examples of how the trick is used.

Simile/Metaphor

Write the definition of each:

    Simile – _____

    Metaphor – _____

Use similes and metaphors to compare each body part listed below.

    Example: His nose is as long as an elephant's trunk.
                 Her nose is hooked like a parrot's.

1. nose – _____

2. ears – _____

3. hair – _____

4. eyes – _____

5. mouth – _____

6. neck – _____

7. body – _____

8. legs – _____

    Below, write a paragraph describing a Metaphor Monster. Then, on a half sheet of paper, draw a picture of your Metaphor Monster.

_____

_____

_____

_____

_____

_____

_____

_____

_____

Hints for Teaching
"Hyperbole"

Before using the worksheet:

It would help tremendously if you found several books that were rich in hyperbole and made a class list of examples. This worksheet can be a chore for the students who are used to being spoon fed answers. It requires a little imagination. Provide some exposure to hyperbole before hand. It will work wonders, and they should quickly get the hang of it. Encourage the students to have fun with the worksheet. Remember, the goal of the worksheet is to get the students to understand that exaggeration is a great way to get a point across.

Beyond the worksheet:

- <u>Writing Assignment:</u> Write a story about a long journey across oceans, over mountains, through terrible storms, and against vicious enemies. Be sure to use hyperbole at least five times.

- <u>Journal:</u> Select five feelings people might experience at a ball game. Describe the feelings using hyperbole.

- <u>Homework:</u> Pick five famous people and describe something they've done using hyperbole.

Writing Trick
Hyperbole

A hyperbole is an exaggeration. Use it when you really want to make a point. There are thousands of ways you can use it. Fill in the blanks with a hyperbole that fits.

Examples

I'm so hungry **I could eat a horse**.

If I don't get a video game for Christmas, **I'll die**.

He ran a **hundred miles an hour**.

1. That dog is so fluffy_____

_____

2. He is so strong _____

_____

3. I'm so happy _____

_____

4. That tiger is so fierce _____

_____

5. Koala bears are so cute _____

_____

6. The whale made such a big splash that _____

_____

7. I'm so thirsty _____

_____

8. The monkey was so silly _____

_____

9. The Doberman barked so loudly _____

_____

10. If I don't get to bed soon _____

_____

11. The odor was so strong _____

_____

12. After dinner, I was so full _____

_____

13. The lamb had enough wool _____

_____

14. That guy was so tough _____

_____

15. Everyone danced for so long _____

_____

Hints for Teaching
"Idioms"

Before using the worksheet:

Explain the definition of an idiom. Use some examples from the worksheet to discuss how most idioms do not make sense if taken literally. However, the meaning of the expression is meant to illustrate a specific point. For example, the expression "To cry wolf" means nothing literally, but if you are familiar with and understand the story about the boy who cried wolf, you know that anyone who gives a false alarm is crying wolf. Also, in boxing, it is not fair to hit below the belt. So, whenever someone acts unfairly, they are said to hit below the belt.

Give the students ten minutes to read through the list of idioms. Have them make a list of five idioms that they DO understand and five idioms that they DO NOT understand. Next, read through the list of idioms, and ask students to explain what they mean. To save time, you can have students ask you to explain the ones that they do not know.

Beyond the worksheet:

Be prepared for the students to use the idioms in ways that don't quite fit. Many students might be unfamiliar with these expressions and may not use them in the proper context. Be patient, and let them have fun with the expressions. Becoming familiar with idioms is the first step to mastery. Have the students make a list of the expressions that they know well enough to use regularly, and add it to their writing folder. It will serve as another reminder of what they are capable of doing. Be sure to give the students plenty of opportunities to use these expressions in their writing.

Writing Trick
Idioms

Directions: Below is a list of idioms and their meanings. Write 15 sentences. Use an idiom in each sentence that fits the meaning of the expression.

Have you ever heard someone say, "Go fly a kite," or "It's as easy as pie?" Well, these are idioms.

An *idiom* is an expression that may, or may not, make sense when you read it. However, it does have a certain meaning when used properly. Idioms give your writing personality. Use this list to practice. Keep your ears open, stay on the ball, and I bet you'll find a bunch more to put into your bag of tricks.

Ace up Your Sleeve = a special advantage that is not used until the very last moment *(Everyone thinks that Rosy will win the contest, but Rachel has <u>an ace up her sleeve.</u>)*

Achilles' Heel = the one weakness or flaw in something or someone that is very strong *(I have no problem staying away from candy, but chocolate is my <u>Achilles' heel</u>.)*

Add Fuel to the Fire = to make a bad situation worse *(The boys were fighting and Tom just <u>added fuel to the fire</u> by making faces.)*

All Ears = ready to listen carefully *(When you're ready to talk, I'm <u>all ears.</u>)*

All Thumbs = clumsy *(It seems like I'm <u>all thumbs</u> because I drop whatever I pick up.)*

Ants in Your Pants = extremely restless; can't sit or stand still *(All of your wiggling makes you look like you've got <u>ants in your pants.</u>)*

At the End of Your Rope = not able to take it any more *(I'm <u>at the end of my rope</u> with all your complaining.)*

Backseat Driver = someone who gives advice that is neither asked for nor wanted *(I can fix my bike by myself. I don't need a <u>backseat driver</u>.)*

Bark Is Worse than Your Bite = to sound more unpleasant or dangerous than one really is *(My dad may yell a lot, but his <u>bark is worse than his bite</u>.)*

Bark Up the Wrong Tree = to give attention to or focus on the wrong thing (*If you think I took your piece of candy, you're <u>barking up the wrong tree</u>.*)

Beat a Dead Horse = to waste energy trying to do something that can't be done. (*You're <u>beating a dead horse</u> if you think the umpire is going to change his call.*)

Birds of a Feather Flock Together = people who have similar interests associate with each other (*All of those kids eating lunch get good grades. <u>Birds of a feather flock together.</u>*)

Bury the Hatchet = to settle an argument or put the past behind you (*When we realized how silly we were acting, Sequoia and I decided to <u>bury the hatchet</u> and be friends again.*)

Busy as a Beaver = working very hard (*I've been as <u>busy as a beaver</u> cleaning up the house.*)

Cost an Arm and a Leg = very expensive (*That car must have <u>cost an arm and a leg</u>.*)

Cry Wolf = to give a false alarm (*There was no fire. Justin was just <u>crying wolf</u>.*)

Cold Feet = lose the desire or nerve to do something (*I thought I could go skydiving, but now that we're up here, I'm getting <u>cold feet</u>.*)

Dead Duck = a person or project that is in big trouble (*When Mom sees that broken window, you're going to be a <u>dead duck</u>.*)

Eating Out of Your Hand = to have control of someone or a group (*My report was so good, the class was <u>eating out of my hand.</u>*)

Eat Your Words = to have to *admit one was mistaken* (*Everyone who said that I would lose had to <u>eat their words</u> when the game was over.*)

Face the Music = accept the punishment for or consequences of an action (*The criminal was brought to the judge to <u>face the music</u>.*)

Fair-Weather Friend = someone who is a friend only when things are going well (*While our pool was being cleaned, all my <u>fair-weathered friends</u> had better things to do than hang out with me.*)

Fix Your Wagon = to get even with someone (*I'm not going to forget about what you did. I'll <u>fix your wagon</u>.*)

Food for Thought = something to think about (*Dad's advice was food for thought.*)

Gets Under Your Skin = to bother or upset tremendously (*When she starts whining, she really gets under my skin.*)

Go Bananas = to go crazy (*When Steven scored the winning touchdown, the crowd went bananas.*)

Go Fly a Kite = to tell someone to go away or to stop bothering you (*I wanted to help my brother, but he told me to go fly a kite.*)

Hard Nut to Crack = a problem that is difficult to solve, or a person who is difficult to reach. (*I tried to make friends with Kim, but she's a hard nut to crack*)

Have a Screw Loose = to behave in a crazy manner (*That driver speeding down the road must have a screw loose.*)

Head Honcho = the person in charge (*As the coach of this team, I'm the head honcho.*)

Hitting Below the Belt = unfair or mean (*John's comment about my weight was hitting below the belt.*)

Hold Your Horses = to be patient (*I couldn't wait to get there, but Dad said, "Hold your horses."*)

In Hot Water = in serious trouble (*If I get an F on this test, I'll be in hot water with my parents.*)

In the Doghouse = to have someone be upset with you (*Since I forgot about Ted's birthday ,I've been in his doghouse.*)

Jump down Your Throat = to react angrily at something someone says or does (*Every time I make a mistake, he jumps down my throat.*)

Keep Your Ear to the Ground = pay attention (*Keep your ear to the ground for when that sale starts.*)

Kicked the Bucket = to die or break down permanently (*My ten year old watch finally kicked the bucket.*)

Lay an Egg = to do poorly (*Those actors <u>laid an egg</u>. The show was horrible.*)

Let the Cat Out of the Bag = to reveal a secret (*Mom accidentally <u>let the cat out of the bag</u> about Dad's birthday present.*)

Lower the Boom = to punish severely (*The judge <u>lowered the boom</u> on the criminal.*)

Make a Mountain out of a Molehill = to turn a small issue into a big issue (*I was only two minutes late. Don't <u>make a mountain out of a molehill</u>.*)

More than One Way to Skin a Cat = there are several ways of doing something (*If I can't earn money mowing lawns, I'll earn it some other way. After all, there's <u>more than one way to skin a cat.</u>*)

Name is Mud = a person who is in trouble (*After what you did, your <u>name is mud</u> at this school.*)

Nitty-Gritty = the main idea of something (*Don't bother me with details. Stick to the <u>nitty-gritty</u>.*)

Nothing to Sneeze At = something which should be treated as important (*Your award for writing is <u>nothing to sneeze at.</u>*)

Off the Hook = no longer in trouble or accountable for (*I thought I had to mow the lawn, but since it rained, I'm <u>off the hook</u>.*)

Off Your Rocker = crazy; foolish (*That teacher must have been <u>off his rocker</u> to give us all that homework.*)

On the Fritz = broken (*Our t.v. has been <u>on the fritz</u> all week.*)

Sight for Sore Eyes = something one is glad to see (*After eating camp food all week, a restaurant was a <u>sight for sore eyes</u>.*)

Tip of the Iceberg = only a hint of a much larger or more complex issue or problem (*For your punishment, you must write fifty sentences, and that's just the <u>tip of the iceberg</u>.*)

Turn Over a New Leaf = to make a fresh start (*Carlos used to be a trouble maker, but he seems to have <u>turned over a new leaf.</u>*)

Wet Blanket = someone who spoils all the fun (*I'm sorry to be a <u>wet blanket</u>, but it's time to go home.*)

Writing Trick
Idioms

Directions: Select any eight idioms, and illustrate them in the boxes below and on the back. Write the definition of the idiom below your picture. When you finish, select your best picture and draw a full sized illustration of it, complete with definition and a sentence.

Writing Trick
Personification #1

Giving human qualities, feelings or actions to objects or animals is called <u>personification</u>.

Example #1: The <u>wind</u> <u>whistled</u> through the trees.

Action: The object "wind" performed the human action of whistling.

Example #2: What a <u>joyful day</u>!

Feeling: The human emotion "joyful" is describing the day.

Directions: In each sentence below, circle the object or animal being personified. Underline the personification. On the line, tell if the personification is an Action or a Feeling.

Example: __action__ The playful (puppy) <u>danced</u> around the room.

_____ 1. The clock said that it was time to go home.

_____ 2. A sad morning began with the news of Kristine's accident.

_____ 3. This old house has a lot of memories.

_____ 4. A video camera witnessed the entire accident.

_____ 5. One lonely flower grew in the middle of a grassy field.

_____ 6. A bird outside my window sang a song just for me.

_____ 7. Our hearts rejoice when we win the game.

_____ 8. Angry rocks of hail pounded on our windshield.

_____ 9. In the tropical forest tiny drops of rain kissed our cheeks.

_____ 10. The sun was hiding behind the clouds.

Writing Trick
Personification #2

Directions: Use the clues below to write sentences using personification.

1. dishes / danced / earthquake
   Example: During the earthquake, the dishes danced across the table.

   _____

   _____

2. proud / flag

   _____

   _____

3. eating into savings / field trips

   _____

   _____

4. smoke / chimney / coughed

   _____

   _____

5. grateful / country

   _____

   _____

6. cling / branch / leaf /

   _____

   _____

7. screamed / fireworks / sky

   _____

   _____

8. marched / ants

   _____

   _____

Writing Trick
Personification #3

Directions: Think of an <u>action</u> or <u>emotion</u> that would personify the following
items. Write a sentence about each item using personification.

Remember: The personification can be a human action or human emotion.

Example:

water: The cool <u>water begged</u> the campers to jump into the lake.

1. leaf: _____

_____

2. clouds: _____

_____

3. chair: _____

_____

4. sun: _____

_____

5. mouse: _____

_____

6. lights: _____

_____

7. kittens: _____

_____

8. door: _____

_____

9. hat: _____

_____

Onomatopoeia #1

Onomatopoeia! What a strange word! Any word that imitates a sound is onomatopoeia. Many times, the writer can invent the spelling of these words. See the examples below.

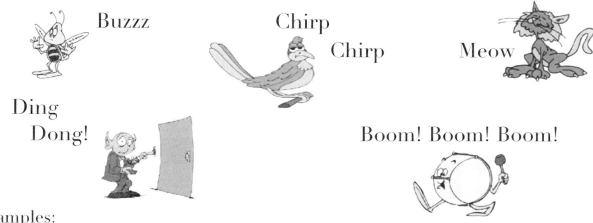

Buzzz   Chirp   Chirp   Meow

Ding Dong!   Boom! Boom! Boom!

Examples:
   The snake <u>hissed</u> as it slithered through the grass.
   <u>Ding dong</u>! The door bell signaled the pizza's arrival.
   The mail carrier stepped into the yard and was greeted with a **grrrr** from Rex.

I. Directions: Make a list of word sounds that might sound like the following:

1. chimes: _____

_____

_____

2. bell: _____

_____

_____

3. baby: _____

_____

_____

4. shoes: _____

_____

_____

5. Angry dog: _____

_____

_____

6. drums: _____

_____

_____

II. Write a sentence using at least one onomatopoeia for each picture above.

Onomatopoeia #2

Directions: Make a list of five (5) sounds that might be heard at each event or situation below. Next, choose three of those sounds, and use each one in a sentence. Remember, you can invent the spelling of any sound you use.

I. Describe an exciting play at a sporting event:

Five Sounds: _____ _____ _____ _____ _____

1. _____

_____

2. _____

3. _____

_____

II. Describe what it is like on a bus that is taking students on a field trip:

Five Sounds: _____ _____ _____ _____ _____

1. _____

_____

2. _____

_____

3. _____

_____

III. Describe the sounds around a dinner table:

Five Sounds: _____ _____ _____ _____ _____

1. _____

_____

2. _____

_____

3. _____

_____

Where / When
Writing Trick #1

What is the Where / When Writing Trick?

This writing trick is a way to make your sentences, stories, and essays more powerful by adding setting. When you explain where and when something is taking place, the reader is able to understand and enjoy your writing on a much deeper level.

Example #1

A bear was searching for food.

Where: in the forest.
When: early one morning

New Sentence:

Early one morning in a beautiful forest a bear was searching for food.

Example #2

Hannibal began the Second Punic War by invading Italy.

Where: crossing the Alps.
When: in 218 B.C.

New Sentence:

In 218 B.C. Hannibal began the Second Punic War by crossing the Alps and invading Northern Italy.

I. Write a phrase for each sentence that explains WHERE and WHEN the action in the sentence takes place.

1. The sprinter raced past three runners to win.

   Where: _____

   When: _____

2. The soldier hid in the bushes and spied on the enemy camp.

   Where: _____

   When: _____

3. The knight battled the dragon to save the beautiful princess.

   Where: _____

   When: _____

4. A medal was placed around the hero's neck.

   Where: _____

   When: _____

5. Smiles stretched across the faces of the proud parents.

   Where: _____

   When: _____

II. On a separate sheet of paper, rewrite the sentences above. Include the phrases that explain WHERE and WHEN the action takes place.

Where / When
Writing Trick
#2

What is the Where / When Writing Trick?

This writing trick is a way to make your sentences, stories, and essays more powerful by adding setting. When you explain where and when something is taking place, the reader is able to understand and enjoy your writing on a much deeper level.

Example 1: A bird chirped happily.

__In the large oak tree outside my room__ a bird chirped happily __on a cool spring morning__.
         (Where)   (When)

Example 2: British ships bombed Fort McHenry for hours.

__Off the shores of Baltimore__ British ships bombed Fort McHenry for hours

__in the early morning of September 14, 1814__ .

I. Directions: Fill in the blanks with a phrase that explains **where** and **when** the action in the sentence takes place.

1. _____ dozens of boys were playing soccer _____

_____ .

2. _____ a wolf _____

howled at the moon.   (Example: At midnight / sitting at the edge of a cliff)

3. A submarine, _____ and _____,

raised its periscope to focus on its target.

4. _____ the pirate looked _____

_____ for the perfect spot to bury his treasure.

5. The racecar driver _____ sped past the leader

_____ to win the race.

6. _____ we set up

   our tent _____.

7. The principal stood at the microphone _____

   ready to address the audience _____.

8. _____ the band marched past

   the crowd _____.

9. The fans _____ cheered as the

   dolphins _____ jumped through the flaming hoops.

10. _____ the lifeguard blew his whistle

    to warn the swimmers _____ to be careful.

II. Directions: On a separate sheet of paper, make up a sentence about each
    picture below. Include a WHERE and WHEN phrase in each sentence.

1.

2.

3.

4.

5.

6.

Follow Up
Writing Trick
Assignments

1. **Writing Trick Review** ... Make a list of writing tricks you've studied along with an example sentence using the trick. Have students select a topic and write sentences about it using each trick three times. I designed this writing assignment for anyone who will miss several days of school and to give to the entire class before major vacations as extra credit to help my students stay sharp.

2. **Writing Trick Stories** ... Put a list of writing tricks on the board. As a journal assignment, homework assignment, or for classroom practice, have your students use them to write stories. The sentences they write must include each writing trick from the list in order. For example, if you put dialogue, adjectives, simile/metaphor, and hyperbole on the board, the students must use dialogue in the first sentence of their stories, adjectives in the second sentence, a simile/metaphor in the third and so on. The example (right) is one of the assignments I give my students. It has worked very well for third graders as well as for adults.

Warm Up
Writing Trick Practice

Directions:
Write a one (1) paragraph letter to a friend. Tell them about something that happened to you last week. Each sentence of the letter must be written using the writing trick listed below. See the sample below if you need help. Skip lines.

Sentence #1 – Attention Getter (Topic Sentence)

Sentence #2 – Show-Not-Tell: Setting (Explain where and when your story takes place.)

Sentence #3 – Adjectives

Sentence #4 – Prepositional Phrase

Sentence #5 – Dialogue

Sentence #6 – Closing Sentence

Example:

February 8, 2008

Dear Joy,

    You'll never believe what happened to me last Wednesday. It was a
(Attention Getter)
beautiful, sunny afternoon with soft, puffy clouds resting against a gentle blue
(Show-Not-Tell: Setting)
sky. I was walking on the playground at recess when I saw a short, brown-
(Adjectives)
haired girl running across the yard. A large, blond-haired girl with a ball under
(prepositional phrase)
her arm, not looking where she was going, was running right toward her. I
yelled, "Watch out! You're going to cra...!" but it was too late. They collided,
(Dialogue)
banged heads and fell to the ground, but they were okay.
(Closing Sentence)

Sincerely,
David

Chapter 6
Helping Your Students
Improve Spelling

This chapter will:

1. Help you improve your students' spelling.

2. Provide procedures to teach spelling.

Introduction:

There is no magic cure-all for teaching students how to spell. There are so many variables involved in learning how to spell that one could spend a lifetime trying to figure it out. I've known many teachers and college professors who have spent years trying to improve their spelling with varying degrees of success. Unfortunately, even the smartest of people need several techniques to show marked improvement. Once the basic phonetic rules of spelling are mastered, there are still many words in the English language that follow their own set of rules. This is why several techniques, other than the basics of phonics, are needed to help improve spelling.

For example, there are several words in English that come from the root word "bene" which means "good". Words such as benefit and benediction are examples. Realizing that the the root "bene" is spelled "b-e-n-e" will prevent common spelling errors such as "benifit". My goal is to give you several techniques that will help build spelling skills. No single technique will work independent of the others.

Spelling Techniques:
1. Spelling List - Plural Rules
2. Daily Spelling Schedule.
3. Spell-Checker
4. Core and Commonly Used Words
5. Flash Cards
6. Student-Teacher Game
7. Root Words Worksheet
8. Rules of Thumb

Spelling Lists (Plurals):

Weekly spelling lists for all grade levels are not difficult to find. Just walk into any teacher supply store, and you'll have your choice of dozens from which to choose. It is for this reason that I will not spend much time trying to recreate what has already been done.

This unit on changing singular words into plurals has made a world of difference in my students' spelling. Most of my fifth graders have seen the rules before, but for whatever reason, they have not retained them. I teach this unit half way through the school year. From that point on, students who break a rule for changing a singular word to plural must write the rule and the word five times. This serves as an excellent motivator for the rest of the class to master the pluralization rules.

SPELLING PLURALS

Rule #1 If a noun ends in "y", preceded by a consonant, change the "y" to "i" and add "es".

country - countries   spy - spies   cry - cries   fly - flies
hobby - hobbies   beauty - beauties   lady - ladies   try - tries
melody - melodies   injury - injuries   sky - skies   copy - copies
mystery – mysteries   berry - berries   supply - supplies

Rule #2 If a noun ends in "y", preceded by a vowel, just add "s" to make the word plural.

chimney – chimneys   turkey – turkeys
valley – valleys   birthday - birthdays   cowboy - cowboys

Rule #3 If a noun ends in "f" or "fe", the "f" or "fe" is usually changed to "v" and "es" is added to make it plural. <u>Chief</u> and <u>belief</u> are two exceptions.

half - halves   thief - thieves   loaf - loaves   life – lives
wolf - wolves   leaf - leaves   self - selves   knife - knives
calf - calves   wife - wives   elf - elves   shelf - shelves

Rule #4 If a noun ends in "o", just "s" is added to make the word plural.

piano - pianos   photo - photos   solo - solos   rodeo - rodeos
banjo - banjos   patio - patios   igloo - igloos

* Sometimes exceptions are made plural by adding "es"

potato - potatoes   tomato - tomatoes   buffalo - buffaloes
tornado – tornadoes   hero - heroes

Rule #5 Some nouns form their plurals in an unusual way.

ox - oxen   foot - feet   tooth - teeth   mouse - mice
child - children   woman - women   goose - geese   deer - deer
sheep - sheep   man - men

Rule #6 If a noun ends in "ss", "x", "z", "sh", or "ch" the suffix "es" is usually added to make it plural.

tax - taxes   branch - branches   glass - glasses   fox - foxes
church - churches   guess - guesses   waltz - waltzes   buzz - buzzes
punch - punches   flash - flashes   hunch - hunches   crutch - crutches
patch - patches   lunch - lunches   bunch - bunches   touch – touches

Name: _____

Spelling Test
Week 1
Rules #1-3

1. hobby - _____

2. half - _____

3. turkey - _____

4. wife - _____

5. fly - _____

6. birthday - _____

7. wolf - _____

8. injury - _____

9. copy - _____

10. calf - _____

11. loaf - _____

12. valley - _____

13. cry - _____

14. melody - _____

15. shelf - _____

16. beauty - _____

17. country - _____

18. self - _____

19. mystery - _____

20. berry - _____

21. knife - _____

22. life - _____

23. cowboy - _____

24. lady - _____

25. thief - _____

26. leaf - _____

27. chimney - _____

28. elf - _____

29. try - _____

30. supply - _____

31. spy - _____

32. sky - _____

Name: _____

Spelling Test
Week 2
Rules #4-6

1. tax - _____

2. piano - _____

3. potato - _____

4. punch - _____

5. touch - _____

6. rodeo - _____

7. foot - _____

8. buzz - _____

9. patio - _____

10. lunch - _____

11. hero - _____

12. patch - _____

13. tooth - _____

14. solo - _____

15. mouse - _____

16. crutch - _____

17. banjo - _____

18. tomato - _____

19. woman - _____

20. guess - _____

21. ox - _____

22. sheep - _____

23. waltz - _____

24. igloo - _____

25. buffalo - _____

26. man - _____

27. bunch - _____

28. goose - _____

29. photo - _____

30. church - _____

31. child - _____

32. branch - _____

33. flash - _____

34. glass - _____

35. deer - _____

36. fox - _____

37. hunch - _____

38. tornado - _____

Spelling Test
Week 3
Rules #1-6

1. hobby - _____
2. half - _____
3. turkey - _____
4. wife - _____
5. fly - _____
6. birthday - _____
7. wolf - _____
8. injury - _____
9. hero - _____
10. patch - _____
11. tooth - _____
12. solo - _____
13. mouse - _____
14. crutch - _____
15. banjo - _____
16. tomato - _____
17. woman - _____

18. country - _____
19. self - _____
20. mystery - _____
21. berry - _____
22. knife - _____
23. life - _____
24. cowboy - _____
25. lady - _____
26. church - _____
27. child - _____
28. branch - _____
29. flash - _____
30. glass - _____
31. deer - _____
32. fox - _____
33. hunch - _____
34. tornado - _____

Daily Spelling Schedule:
First Semester

Spelling Routine
1st Semester

Day 1 - Pretest / Correct the Pretest / Divide words into Syllables
   H.W.: Write your spelling words 3 x's each.

Day 2 - Spell Checker - "Look, Say, Cover, Check, Write, Look"
- Look: Look at the words and underline the tricky parts. Next, divide the words that you missed into syllables.
- Say: Say the word several times.
- Cover: Cover the word and spell it out loud.
- Check: Check to see if you spelled it correctly.
- Write: Write the word.
- Look: Look to see if you spelled it correctly.

Day 3 - Select any 5 words and do the following:
A. Dictionary Skills:
   1. Look up the word and write the two guide words.
   2. Write the entry word (spelling word), phonetic spelling, other forms of the word, and their part of speech.
   3. Alphabetize the five words.
Example: Entry word: fluent
      Guide Words: flower - forward
      Phonetic Spelling: (flu' ent)
      Other Forms: fluently (Adverb)
H.W.: Any worksheets from the language arts book.

Day 4 - Student Teacher Game

Day 5 Test: Turn in Spelling Work

Monday Paper Set Up:
   1. Front = Pretest / Spell Checker   Back = 3 X's Each
   2. Front = Dictionary Skills   Back = Student / Teacher Game
   3. Add any worksheets.
      Staple together. Turn in on Friday.

For a spelling program to work, it must be done consistently. Also, because there are so many topics to teach during our language arts time, having a spelling program that makes the most of every minute is a big advantage.

On the left is a picture of my classroom's spelling schedule. This schedule not only helps the students master the spelling concept of the week, it also helps meet several other standards. In addition to learning spelling words, students practice syllabication, dictionary skills, alphabetizing, prefixes / suffixes, and writing skills.

With these routines students know what to expect every day. By the third week of school, they automatically begin to work on their spelling with a minimum of teacher direction. Little time is wasted, and the fifteen to twenty minutes spent are used efficiently.

In my class, students work on spelling during Smart Start, the time when they first enter the classroom and work on spelling, grammar, and journal writing. Day 1, 2, 3, 4, and 5 is simply a pacing guide. Students who complete the list are welcome to use their extra time for other activities such as silent reading, homework, or math practice. It is quite common to have several students working on other activities on Day 4 while the others are playing the Student-Teacher review game.

Here is how the weekly spelling program works:
(All the student worksheets follow the explanation of the eight steps below.)

Day 1 –
1st Semester – Pretest / Check Pretest / Divide Words into Syllables
2nd Semester – Pretest / Check Pretest / 3 Vocabulary Words

Begin the spelling unit by giving a pretest. This provides students the opportunity to see how well they know the words of the week. It also prepares them for the spelling tasks you will assign. Most school districts have spelling lists specific to each grade level. For home school teachers, contact your local school for a list that fits your needs. If you have a list of recommended words for your students' grade level, add three words from the list to your words of the week. If you prefer, you can add words from other subjects. For example, in science you might add "photosynthesis" or "biodegradable"

Follow the same procedure for giving the pretest as you do for giving the spelling test:

A. Say the word, say the word in a sentence, say the word again.
B. Correct the pretest. The students are to point to each letter as you spell the word. Make them put a dot above the letter as you say it so you know they are following along. They may circle any parts of the word where they spelled incorrectly.

You may want to consider an alternate assignment for students who regularly make a perfect score on their pretest. One suggestion is to have these students work on writer's workshop activities.

Check Pretest / Pronounce the spelling words together.

If students cannot pronounce a word, it's going to be nearly impossible for them to spell, and they certainly won't be using it in their writing. Therefore, give your students some time to practice pronouncing the words. Follow these steps:

A. Say the word, and have the students repeat it after you.

B. Each spelling unit normally focuses on a "Rule." Point out the current week's spelling rule. Ask students to identify words that follow the rule of the week and words that follow rules previously studied. For example, if the current spelling unit focuses on the "ou" sound, ask, "Which word has the 'ou' sound as in 'round'? Which word has the 'ou' sound as in 'wound (an injury)'?"

C. Review the definitions of any words they may find difficult.

D. In pairs, have students practice saying the words to each other.

1st Semester – Syllables   /   2nd Semester – Root Words

Federal standards require most grade levels to practice syllabication and to study the roots of English words. This spelling routine allows you to teach these standards within your spelling unit, saving precious class time for other standards.

During the first semester, the students will follow up their pretest by dividing the words into syllables. Next, have them circle (better yet, have them use a highlighter – the students love using highlighters) the syllables they misspelled. This will make the Day 2 activity, Spell Checker, much easier.

During the second semester, I add a root word to the spelling list along with two or three words that contain that root. For example, I use the root "bene", meaning "good". I add "benefit" and "benefactor" to the spelling list. A mini-lesson helps students see how the root word "bene" fits into the definitions of these words and many others. "bene", meaning "good". I would add "benefit" and "benefactor" to the spelling list. A mini-lesson would help the students see how the root word "bene" fits into the definitions of these words and many others. For an excellent list of root words, look for English from the Roots Up by Joegil K. Lundquist. You can also find a list of root words at *CreateBetterWriters.com* in the "Past Newsletters" section of the website.

Day 2 "Spell Checker" - "Look, Say, Cover, Check, Write, Look" /
H.W. for Day 1, 2nd Semester.

Give your students the "Spell Checker" worksheet, and go over it with them. It explains how this step works. After three or four weeks, they will use it with very little direction from you.

Emphasize the following regarding this step:

First, remind them that a syllable contains <u>one vowel sound</u>. After they divide a word into syllables, they are to say the word and clap after each syllable. My students have learned to do this when they see words with several syllables in their reading. Taking the time to do this step correctly also improves reading skills.

Next, have them underline or highlight any tricky parts in each word. For example, if students spell the word "rhythm" - "r-i-t-h-m", they would underline "rhy" to focus their attention on that part of the word. This technique helps identify patterns in words. In time, students will find they underline fewer and fewer letters as they learn to identify the patterns in words.

The rest of the Spell Checker technique is meant to help students master the entire list of words. If your students are not making almost perfect scores, and you are providing a reasonable amount of study time, the spelling list may be too long.

A to Z *Spell Checker* A to Z

Look
* *Divide the word into syllables.*
* *Look for any part of the word that is* **Tricky**.
Say
* *Say the word, one syllable at a time.*
Cover
* *Cover the word and spell it outloud. Do this one syllable at a time until you can spell the entire word.*
Check
* *Check to see if you spelled the word correctly.*
* *If you couldn't, look at what tricked you and try again.*
Write
* *Spell the word on paper.*
Look
* *Look to see if you spelled it correctly.*
* *If you didn't spell the word correctly, return to the top and repeat the Spell Checker.*

2ⁿᵈ Semester – By the 2nd semester, students understand Spell Checker well enough to use it independently for homework. Therefore, in class, have students practice their writing tricks (Ch. 5) with the spelling words. The trade off for the students is that they no longer have to write each spelling word three times.

For homework, the students will complete the Root Word worksheet. On this worksheet, students record the root word, its Latin or Greek definition, two words derived from the root and their definitions. Then, they draw study pictures (see Picture Dictionary in Ch. 4) to learn the new words.

Day 3 – 1ˢᵗ Semester: Dictionary Skills / 2ⁿᵈ Semester: Prefixes and Suffixes

Dictionary Skills – As stated on the worksheet, students learn to use guide words, to read the phonetic spelling used in dictionaries, and to look for other forms of the word.

Prefixes and Suffixes – Here, students learn to make new words using prefixes and suffixes. Some units, such as one in which the spelling list consists solely of proper nouns, don't lend themselves to this activity. While it doesn't happen often, when it does, simply skip this activity or add three words to the spelling list that would support this activity.

Homework – The homework for both semesters is to complete any worksheets that came with the spelling list. Most language arts series include a few worksheets to accompany the list.

Day 4 - Play "Student / Teacher Game"

This game was designed as a practice test but also works well as a peer tutoring activity. I pair students who struggle with spelling with someone who does well. As they take turns spelling words, those who struggle see how a peer spells a word and receive advice from someone at their level. Sometimes adults will explain a concept multiple times, and children cannot understand it. However, a peer can explain exactly the same thing in the exactly the same way and the same children will grasp it right away. For an explanation of how the student / teacher game works, see Chapter 4.

Day 5 - Take the Test

Spelling Routine
1st Semester

Day 1 – Pretest / Correct the Pretest / Divide words into Syllables

    H.W. Write your spelling words 3 x's each.

Day 2 – Spell Checker - "Look, Say, Cover, Check, Write, Look"

- <u>Look</u>: Look at the words and underline the tricky parts. Next, divide the words that you missed into syllables.
- <u>Say</u>: Say the word several times.
- <u>Cover</u>: Cover the word and spell it out loud.
- <u>Check</u>: Check to see if you spelled it correctly.
- <u>Write</u>: Write the word.
- <u>Look</u>: Look to see if you spelled it correctly.

Day 3 – Select any 5 words and do the following:

    A. Dictionary Skills:

        1. Look up the word and write the two <u>guide words</u>.

        2. Write the entry word (spelling word), phonetic spelling, other forms of the word, and their part of speech.

        3. Alphabetize the five words.

    Example: <u>Entry word:</u> fluent

                <u>Guide Words</u>: flower - forward

                <u>Phonetic Spelling</u>: (flu' ent)

                <u>Other Forms</u>: fluently (Adverb)

    H.W. Any worksheets from the language arts book.

Day 4 – Student Teacher Game

Day 5 Test: Turn in Spelling Work

Monday Paper Set Up:

    1.   Front = Pretest / Spell Checker   Back = 3 X's Each

    2.   Front = Dictionary Skills   Back = Student / Teacher Game

    3.   Add any worksheets.

            Staple together. Turn in on Friday.

Spelling Routine
2nd Semester

Day 1 – Pretest / Correct the Pretest / Start Spell Checker

<u>Add Root Word and 3 Vocabulary Words to Your List</u>

H.W. Spell Checker - "Look, Say, Cover, Check, Write, Look"

- <u>Look</u>: Look at the words and underline the tricky parts. Next, divide the words that you missed into syllables.
- <u>Say</u>: Say the word several times.
- <u>Cover</u>: Cover the word and spell it out loud.
- <u>Check</u>: Check to see if you spelled it correctly.
- <u>Write</u>: Write the word. • <u>Look</u>: Look to see if you spelled it correctly.

Day 2 – Select any five words and <u>write five sentences using writing tricks</u>. You may not use any writing trick more than once.

Example: routine

<u>Compound Sentence</u>: We have a spelling <u>routine</u> in our class, and I follow it every week.

Writing Tricks: Adjectives, Dialogue, Compound Sentence Ly-How Adverb, Prepositional Phrase, Complex Sentence, Compound-Complex Sentence, Simile/Metaphor, Appositives, Phrases in a List, Onomatopoeia, Idioms, Vaunting Verbs, Hyperbole

H.W. Root-words Worksheet

Day 3 – Prefixes and Suffixes

A. Prefixes: Select any three (3) words and add a prefix. You have just made a new word. Write the new definition next to your new words.

Example: certain / uncertain - not sure.

B. Suffixes: Select any three (3) words and add a suffix. You have just changed the part of speech. Write the new words and their new parts of speech.

Example: prompt / promptly - Adverb

H.W. Any worksheets from the language arts book.

Day 4 – Student Teacher Game

Day 5 Test: Turn in Spelling Work

Friday, Turn In:
1. Front = Pretest / Spell Checker   Back = Writing Tricks
2. Front = Prefixes / Suffixes   Back = Student / Teacher Game
3. Root Words Worksheet and any other worksheets.

Look

* Divide the word into syllables.
* Look for any part of the word that is **Tricky**.

Say

* Say the word, one syllable at a time.

Cover

* Cover the word and spell it outloud. Do this one syllable at a time until you can spell the entire word.

Check

* Check to see if you spelled the word correctly.
* If you couldn't, look at what tricked you and try again.

Write

* Spell the word on paper.

Look

* Look to see if you spelled it correctly.
* If you didn't spell the word correctly, return to the top and repeat the Spell Checker.

Root Words

Root Word - _____ Greek / Latin

Definition - _____

_____

2 Words:	Definition
1. _____ -	_____
	_____
2. _____ -	_____
	_____

Picture Dictionary

Root Word	Word #1	Word #2

Words in a Sentence

1. _____

_____

2. _____

_____

Rules of Thumb

Here are some spelling rules that are hard to find. They come in handy on some of the tricky words. Give them to your students when you feel they are ready to handle them.

1. General rules for *-ly*

    A. Add *ly* after the root word even if it ends in a silent *e*.
        Example: really, scarcely, certainly, crudely
      Exceptions are: true (truly), due (duly), whole (wholly), simple (simply)

    B. If a word ending in *y* has a long *e* sound, drop the *y* and change it to *i* before adding *ly*.
        Example: happy + *ly* = happily

    C. If an adjective ends in *-ble*, drop the *e* and add *y*
        Example: comfortable + *ly* = comfortably

2. General rules for *-ous*

    A. Add *ous* to most words ending in a consonant.
        Examples: humor + *ous* = humorous ; danger + *ous* = dangerous

    B. If the word ends with *f*, then change the *f* to a *v* and add *ous*.
        Examples: grief + *ous* = grievous ; mischief + *ous* = mischievous

    C. If a word ends in a silent *e*, drop the *e* and add *ous*.
        Example: continue + *ous* = continuous

    D. If a word ends in a soft *c*, change the *e* to *i* and add *ous*.
        Examples: space + *ous* = spacious ; grace + *ous* = gracious

    E. If a word ends in *y* preceded by a consonant, change the *y* to *i* and add *ous*.
        Example: vary + ous = various

3. *-able* vs. *-ible*

    A The ending should be *-able*:
        * If the base word is a full word. Ex. accept = acceptable
        * If the base word is a full word except for the final *e*. Ex. desire = desirable
        * If the base word ends in *i*. Ex. envy = enviable
        * If the base word ends in a hard *c* or *g*. Ex. despicable, navigable

    B. The ending should be *-ible*:
        * If the base word is not a full word. Ex. permissible ; possible
        * If the base word ends in *ns*. Ex. responsible
        * If you can add *-ion* to the base word. Ex. collect, collection, collectible
        * If the base word ends in a soft *c* or *g*. Ex. convincible, illegible

Chapter 7
Putting It
All Together

This chapter will:

1. Show you how to use your bulletin boards as teaching tools.

2. Help keep the newly learned writing skills fresh in your students' minds.

3. Generate ideas for the layout of your learning environment.

4. Provide a year long schedule to make the most of all the writing techniques in this book.

Visual Layout of the Learning Environment

Bulletin Boards as Teaching Tools

For many, if a new skill is out of sight, it's out of mind. This is the case for many of my students. It is so frustrating to teach a wonderful writing concept only to see it ignored the day after I stop focusing on it. So how do we get our students to incorporate the skills they've learned into their writing on a consistent basis? I try to keep the most important skills I've taught on display for as long as possible. Only when I feel that a concept has been mastered, and is being used regularly, do I replace it with another. This is a sample of what my students see every day as they work on their writing. You will notice many of the activities from the lessons in this book on my bulletin boards. Feel free to follow my design or get as creative as you wish.

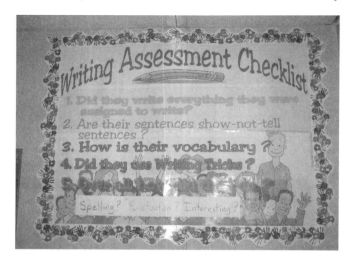

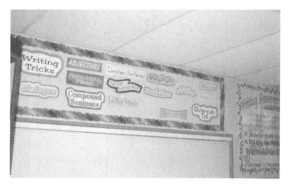

These pictures show what my students see every day as they work on their writing. These are the concepts they've been learning all year. The bulletin boards help keep the concepts fresh in their minds as they work.

The Writing Assessment Checklist poster is easy to make on any graphics program. Make it on one sheet of paper. Many printers allow you to print 2x2, 3x3, etc… Mine measures 4x4, and it takes up a lot of wall space. However, it is impossible for the students to ignore. The students use it throughout the year so it is easy to justify the space.

The pictures on the right show the writing tricks and show-not-tell strategies that we've learned during the year. You can write the name of the tricks on sentence strips or make nice, colorful graphics on your word processor.

The show-not-tell and writing trick bulletin boards serve as excellent reminders for the students. While working on writing assignments they have a handy reference of all of the skills they've learned. Whatever you use, it is important to have some sort of visual reminder to help the student keep the many skills they learn fresh in their minds.

Keeping a Writing Folder

The goal of this program is to develop well-rounded writers for whom great writing is second nature while realizing that perfection is never achieved. As with so many other skills, the day my students stop using a writing skill they've learned is the day they begin to loose it.

Therefore, I've created a writing folder where my students keep their work for the year. They use it as a reference while they work on writing projects and as a review for homework assignments that ask them to practice skills taught weeks or months in the past. I encourage my students to keep it with them even as they pass from grade to grade. Their future teachers may not use words like "writing tricks" and "show-not-tell", but my students will recognize them just the same.

Here is how I organize my students' writing folders:

 Each student should use a three ring binder (1") and dividers. Encourage students to buy their own so that they can take it with them to the next grade. Once they've been trained in this writing program, it is not uncommon for students to save their folders for several years. Several of my students have returned to show me that they still have and use their writing folders and how they've added to them each year.

Below is a description of each section of the folder and the worksheets that should go into it. Insert the worksheets, and label each section while discussing the purpose of each one. Some worksheets are found in the chapters; however, most of them are in the appendix.

Section 1: Writing
"Writing"
"Individual Writing Assessment Sheet"
"Writing Proofs"
"Scoring Sheet"
* This section is used when
  students to score each other's
  writing.

Section 2: Show-Not-Tell
"Show-not-Tell"
* Keep all the show-not-tell lessons in this
  section.

Section 3: Vocabulary
"Vocabulary"
"Vocabulary Words I Like" - The students
 keep a list of their favorite words here.
* They keep their picture dictionaries and
  Let Me Count The Ways worksheets here.

Section 4: Writing Tricks
"Writing Tricks"
* Students keep all the writing trick
  worksheets they've done in this section for
  future reference.

Section 5: Writing Goal - In November/December, administer a writing assessment. Use the results to help your students set a writing goal for the year. They record their goal in this section and a paragraph explaining what they need to do to reach their goal. Their paragraph should include one sentence for each item on the writing assessment checklist. Am I writing everything I am supposed to write? How are my sentences? Vocabulary? Writing Tricks? and Overall? Each month, they should review the contents of their folders and write a new explanation of how they are progressing.

A Sample Lesson Plan
for the First Year of Writing

I've given so much information that you may not know where to begin. Here is a sample of how my year of writing works. Parents who home school are fortunate to have the opportunity to complete the program and utilize it to its fullest potential. Good luck and feel free to adjust the program to fit the needs of your students.

First Month
* Teach the Writing Tricks - "Adjectives" and "Dialogue" (Ch. 5)
* Teach Show-not-Tell "Setting" (Ch. 3)
* Begin Let Me Count the Ways and Root Words vocabulary program. (Ch. 4)
* Master the paragraph.
    ** Be sure to give homework practice on writing tricks, paragraph work, and
       show-not-tell.

Second Month
* Teach Writing Tricks - "Simile/Metaphor" and "Onomatopoeia" (Ch. 5)
* Teach Show-not-Tell "Scared" (Ch. 3)
* Finish mastering the paragraph.
* Give a 45/60 minute timed writing assessment. (See Appendix)

Third Month
* Teach students the Writing Assessment Checklist and how to assess each other's writing.
  (Ch. 1)
* Assess all writing assignments and complete the writing process. (Ch. 1)
* Give writing goal. (Ch. 1 and 7)
    ** Continue with vocabulary and homework practice with writing tricks and show-not-tell.

Fourth Month
* Teach Writing Tricks - "Prepositional Phrase" and "Appositives"
* Teach Show-not-Tell "Excited"
* Complete a writing assignment where the writing process is completed. Be sure to assess the
  rough drafts. Make up a writing assignment that is related to the reading you are doing or
  select one from the Appendix.
* Give a 45/60 minute timed writing assignment. See Appendix for prompts.
    ** Remember to give regular homework assignments which reviews the writing tricks
       and show-not-tell lessons. (Ch. 3 and 5)

Fifth Month
* Teach Writing Tricks- "Phrases in a Series" and "Introductory Phrase" (Ch.5)
* Begin work on the three paragraph essay.
* Assess a three paragraph essay. (Ch.1)
* Give a 45-60 minute timed writing assignment. (See Appendix)

Sixth Month
* Teach Writing Tricks- "Vaunting Verbs" and "Ly How Adverbs" (Ch. 5)
* Continue practice on the three paragraph essay.
* Teach Show-not-Tell "Sad" (Ch. 3)
* Complete a writing assignment where the writing process is completed. Be sure to assess the rough drafts. Make the assignment something related to what you are reading in class or select one from Ch. 8.
** Remember to give regular homework assignments reviewing the writing tricks and show-not-tell. (Ch. 3 and 5)

Seventh and Eighth Month
* By now your students know at least twelve writing tricks and four show-not-tell techniques.
* Write three-five paragraph essays in all subjects: science, reading, and social studies.
* Continue assessing each other's assignments.
* Do a 45-60 minute timed writing assignment. (See Appendix)

Ninth Month
* In the ninth month, I emphasize the fact that they are going to take a writing test to determine if they make their writing goal in the next few weeks. Because you've been assessing their writing all year, they know how close they are to achieving their goal. Many students may be consistently making scores on their writing that show they are meeting their goal. Therefore, I spend this month practicing the writing process, writing tricks, and show-not-tell.

Tenth Month
* Final practice on the writing process and preparation for their writing test.
* Writing Test. Write to a prompt. 60 minutes. (See Appendix)
* Celebration for those who make their writing goal.

Chapter 8

Extras

This chapter will:

1. Help you teach your students how to write a story.

2. Give samples of writing activities you can do with your students.

3. Give projects that will reinforce the concepts taught in this book.

Story Writing
(Domain of Writing: Narrative)

Here are two ways to teach story writing. The first one takes several weeks, but you get to teach so many concepts while you teach it that it is worth the time. Once the students understand what it takes to write a story, teach them the shorter version, and put them to work. As a result, they will write several stories during the year and strengthen their writing skills with each one.

A. Story Writing: The Long Version
** See the lesson plan for "Scary Story" in the following pages for a day-to-day lesson plan for writing these kinds of stories.

Step 1: Begin by teaching the <u>elements of a story.</u>
(This also helps tremendously during reading lessons.)
A. Give the students the definitions of each element of a story. Write them on an overhead or the chalkboard for the students to copy. (See Appendix for master sheet with definitions.)
B. Read a story with your class. Identify each element of the story - introduction, conflict, rising action, climax, resolution, and epilogue.

C. Have the students memorize the elements of a story and continue to discuss them during reading lessons.

Elements of a Story
Introduction
Conflict
Rising Action
Rising Action
Rising Action
Climax
Resolution
Epilogue

Story Writing
* Use this worksheet to help plan your story. Fill in the information below:

Theme:
_____

Introduction: _____

Conflict: _____

Rising Action:

    #1. _____

    #2. _____

    #3. _____

Climax: _____

Epilogue:_____

* Cluster each section of the story.
* Add show-not-tell where needed.
* Write your paragraphs.
* Revise and edit your story.
* Write your final draft and illustrate your story.

Step 2: Sketching the story.
A. Select the topic for the writing assignment.
B. Have the students vote on a theme (a lesson that can be learned from the story). Next, use the theme to select possible conflicts for your story. Once the conflict is chosen, vote on a resolution for that conflict.
C. Have students write the theme, conflict, and resolution on their story sketch.
D. Fill in the rest of the story sketch by choosing the introduction, rising actions, a climax, and an epilogue that fit the conflict and resolution you created.

Step 3: Pre-writing and Rough Draft

Now that the story is sketched out, the students are ready to pre-write. Each element of the story will become one paragraph. Each element from the worksheet will be used as the center of a cluster. As a class, think of five to six sentences which describe how each element of the story will take place. For example, the Introduction of the story might say: "Tim and Elizabeth arrive at school for a Halloween party." Write this sentence in the center of a cluster. Then, around the cluster, write five or six sentences describing the event taking place.

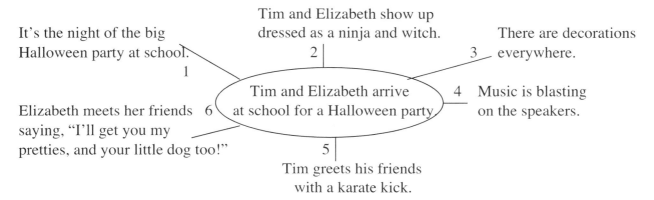

It's the night of the big Halloween party at school.
1

Tim and Elizabeth show up dressed as a ninja and witch.
2

There are decorations everywhere.
3

Tim and Elizabeth arrive at school for a Halloween party

Music is blasting on the speakers.
4

Elizabeth meets her friends saying, "I'll get you my pretties, and your little dog too!"
6

Tim greets his friends with a karate kick.
5

Now, you have a few choices. You can cluster all the elements of the story at once, and then write the paragraphs. The second option is to cluster the elements and write their paragraphs one at a. The third option is to cluster two elements at a time, and then write their paragraphs. This works well when you want your students to write one paragraph in class and write the other paragraph for homework. Whatever option you choose, when the students pre-write their paragraphs, require that they use at least two writing tricks in each paragraph.

Either before starting the story or after you've written the Introduction and the Climax, teach show-not-tell: setting, show-not-tell: scared, and a writing trick. Notice that the items in the cluster give the students a chance to describe the setting of the party. The show-not-tell: setting lesson will help them write an intelligent paragraph that introduces the characters and the setting of the story <u>before</u> they begin the heart of the story. Next, by teaching a writing trick while writing the scary storied, the students get a chance to apply their new skill in a fun, practical assignment. Finally, since this is a scary story, someone in the story should be getting frightened. This is the best time to teach the show-not-tell: scared lesson. Then they can add a paragraph to their story, showing one of their characters being scared.

After you add show-not-tell paragraphs, the story will be nearly ten paragraphs long, and you may see it as an awesome undertaking. However, I have taught these lessons to hundreds of students and can assure you I have had very few complaints about the length of this assignment. Creating the story is so much fun story that most of my students are very eager to work.

Step 4: First Edit

Editing eleven paragraphs by thirty students can be a daunting challenge. Send notes home for the parents to help correct spelling and punctuation. Edit a few paragraphs yourself, including the first paragraph, the conflict, and the show-not-tell paragraphs. Then have the students trade papers with each other.

The students will assess each others' writing using the Writing Assessment Checklist. Provide a list of items, on the board or as a handout, to check while they edit such as: indented paragraphs, capitalization (first word of a sentences and proper nouns), complete sentences, parts of the story that don't make sense. Students may find it helpful to check off each item as it is assessed. When they receive their score, they can practice editing

Step 5: Revising

The students read the suggestions made by their classmates and comments of the teacher. They are required to do the following:
    A. Fix any parts of the story that do not make sense.
    B. Make sure each paragraph has two writing tricks.
    C. Use a thesaurus to change at least one word in each paragraph into a strong vocabulary word.
    ** D. Ask yourself, "Is there any part of the story that I could rewrite so that it paints a better picture?
        ** I challenge the stronger writers, who typically finish before the other students, to photocopy descriptive paragraphs from books. I ask these students read the paragraphs, discuss the descriptive parts, and then rewrite sections of their story.

Step 6: Final Edit and Final Draft

As mentioned earlier, the students read their story with a parent and do a final edit. Once they are convinced that their story is as good as it can be, they begin writing their final draft. Use the book paper provided in the Appendix, or have them use regular notebook paper. I have my students illustrate their stories and to design book jackets that resemble those they would find on a brand new book. Each cover must include a price tag, bar codes, illustrations, title, author, awards, book summary, "about the author" summary, and any other creative items they may want.

Scary Story
Lesson Plan

Before starting this lesson, teach show-not-tell <u>setting</u>.

Day 1

Have students fill out the Scary Story sheet. Put this on the board:

Samples: Don't take candy from strangers. (Or) Obey your parents.	A kid is kidnapped and taken to Dracula's castle (or) A kid trick or treats without parents permission.	graveyard	vampire
Themes "Lessons"	Conflicts "Problems"	Settings	Characters

- ➢ Divide the class into groups of four.
- ➢ Have the students copy the four items above on a piece of paper.
- ➢ Give them 15 minutes to think of ideas. After 15 minutes, one person from each group writes their best ideas in the columns.
- ➢ Vote on the best theme as a class. Then, as a class, select a conflict based on the theme. Students may choose their own if they like.
- ➢ Give the students the Story Writing worksheet. They write the class theme and conflict on that paper.

Day 2

- ➢ Review the theme and conflict.
- ➢ Select a resolution.
- ➢ Students fill out the rest of the Story Writing worksheet.

Day 3

- ➢ Cluster and write the introduction paragraph. Include a show-not-tell description of the setting, and introduce the characters.

Day 4

- ➢ Teach Writing Trick - Simile / Metaphor.

Day 5

- ➢ Cluster and write the conflict paragraph. Cluster the Rising Action #1 paragraph (The conflict gets worse.) Write this paragraph for homework.

Day 6

- ➢ Show-Not-Tell Scared Lesson

Day 7
- ➢ Write a show-not-tell: scared paragraph about a character in the story becoming afraid.

Day 8
- ➢ Cluster and write Rising Action #2 and #3 paragraphs. Be sure to include 2 Adjective Writing Tricks, 2 Dialogue, 2 Simile/Metaphor and 2 Onomatopoeia.

Day 9
- ➢ Cluster and write the Climax and Resolution paragraphs.

Day 10
- ➢ Cluster and write the Epilogue paragraph.

Day 11
- ➢ Write 3 sentences summarizing the story.
- ➢ As students finish, they can put a ruler in their pocket chart, or their names on the board to signal that they are finished and ready to edit.
- ➢ Students who are finished: Do Round Table Editing in groups of 4.
- ➢ They should highlight possible spelling and punctuation errors.
- ➢ If there are errors to be corrected, tell the authors.

Day 12
- ➢ Correct mistakes and revise stories. Add: 3 strong vocabulary words, 3 writing tricks, and 3 show-not-tell setting sentences.
- ➢ All students finish and peer edit the rough drafts.

Day 13
- ➢ Start final drafts on book paper. Illustrate them for homework. Three paragraphs are due tomorrow.

Day 14
- ➢ Finish final drafts and illustrations. Finished final draft is due tomorrow.

Day 15
- ➢ Work on illustrations and make the cover.

Story Writing: The Short Version
Growth Stories (How to Develop a Story)

Whether your students are writing an epic such as War and Peace, or a short fable like "The Fox and the Grapes", their stories must have an introduction, a conflict, some action, a climax and a resolution.

The growth stories begin much the same way as the longer stories. You can decide on the conflict or resolution first by using the Story Writing sheet, or you can allow the students to let the story to develop on its own.

Step 1:

Once the students understand the elements of a story, they simply have to write one or two sentences for each element.

Elements of a Story
Introduction
Conflict
Rising Action
Rising Action
Rising Action
Climax
Resolution
Epilogue

Introduction: This should include details about the setting and the characters.

Conflict: Present the problem the character(s) must solve. Keep it to one to two sentences.

Rising Action: There should be at least three. Even in a short story such as this, if the conflict is resolved too quickly, the story will be boring. Therefore, there should be at least three attempts at solving the conflict.

Rising Action #1 - The conflict gets worse.
Rising Action #2 - Some progress is made towards resolving the conflict.
Rising Action #3 - The conflict is almost solved.

Climax: The major turning point in the story where the conflict's resolution is uncertain.

Resolution: The conflict is resolved.

Epilogue: One sentence conclusion.

Sample Story: You can read this to your students, and have them find the elements of the story. Use it to help explain how to write these growth stories. Do this on the first day because it's the most time consuming step. Steps two and three can be done on the following day(s).

The Beach Attack

Shawn was lying on the beach when suddenly, a blast of water hit him in the face. "What in the world was that?!" he shouted.

Shawn turned around just in time to see two female heads duck behind a surf board stuck in the sand.

Determined that revenge would be his, Shawn picked up his cup of pudding which he knew would look real good all over their heads.

There, Shawn was met with a flurry of water balloons.

He raced back to his towel with four girls on his heels.

Suddenly, his friends raced in front him fully armed with their own bucket of water balloons.

With a sudden u-turn, Shawn was back in the action.

All of a sudden, both sides were out of ammunition and, everyone was ready for hand to hand combat.

"Break it up you guys," came Dad's voice.

The water war was over for now.

Step 2:

Now that the basic elements of the story are there, the students can make this simple story grow by adding more details to it. Simply add one sentence to each element of the story. The sentences should ADD information to the story and should be natural. Write a story with your students, and do this step with them. They should get the idea pretty quickly. Also, you can use the story on the right. Step 2 is in italics. Leave it out, (or use it as a guide if they struggle) and have the class generate ideas.

The Beach Attack

Shawn was lying on the beach when suddenly, a blast of water hit him in the face. "What in the world was that?!" he shouted.

Shawn turned around just in time to see two female heads duck behind a surfboard stuck in the sand. *Those girls are going to pay for that, he thought.*

Determined that revenge would be his, Shawn picked up his cup of pudding, which he new would look real good all over their heads. *Quickly, he raced behind the surf board.*

There, Shawn was met with a flurry of water balloons. *It was an ambush. He had to get out of there.*

He raced back to his blanket with four girls on his heals. *They all had a big, juicy water balloon in each hand.*

Suddenly, his friends raced in front him fully armed with their own bucket of water balloons. *"Get ready for a slaughter, girls!" yelled Joey who lived for water balloon fights.*

With a sudden u-turn, Shawn was back in the action. *Balloons flying everywhere, Shawn found a nice red one and searched for his first victim.*

All of a sudden, both sides were out of ammunition and they were all ready for hand-to-hand combat. *Shawn stared at Kari, who had an evil smile. She had been the one who had surprised him, and she would be the one wearing this pudding in about five seconds.*

"Break it up you guys," came Dad's voice. *"It's time for cake and ice cream. You can kill each other later."*

The water war was over for now. *Shawn was determined that he would not be the first victim in another such attack. He would be the one to strike first.*

Step 3:

The final step is to add information to the story to make it even more interesting. Include show-not-tell setting and emotions. A description of the beach or the water balloon fights would be great. Show-not-tell descriptions of how Shawn felt about being hit by the water balloon or what he looked like would add depth to the story.

Using writing tricks to change sentences is an effective strategy for students to employ. Depending on the ability level of the students, they may or may not have used many writing tricks in their original version of the story.

Finally, other changes could include giving the characters unusual names, changing the title, or adding more details in the same manner as in step #3.

Letter Writing
(A Lesson Plan)

Introduction:

Make letter writing second nature for your students with this lesson plan. I have found it very effective in helping my students master the basics of letter writing. Teach the friendly letter format first because it is easy to learn. Once students master the friendly letter, they have the confidence to write a business letter which takes just a few more steps to compose. As always, learning a new skill requires practice.

The Friendly Letter

Begin by explaining that a mnemonic device is a <u>memory</u> aid. It is a trick to help memorize important information or remember the order of something by making it fun! Then teach your students this trick. In minutes they will have memorized the five parts of the friendly letter for a life time. I once introduced this trick at the beginning of the school year for use in a simple assignment. Months later, when I began our formal lessons on letter writing, many of the students remembered it. The five parts of a friendly letter are: **Heading, Greeting, Body, Closing, and Signature**

The Memory Trick

Display a sample of a friendly letter on the board or on a poster. Point to your head, mouth, body, skirt/pants/shorts, and foot as you point to and explain the parts of a letter. Students will stand, and, as you point to and name the parts of a letter, they will follow your example. Review the parts several times, slowly at first. The fun begins when, as you call out the parts faster and faster, the students try to keep up.

Heading:

Obviously, pointing to the head symbolizes "Heading." Tell your students that your head is the top of your body, and the heading is the top of a letter. Point to the drawing of a friendly letter to show them where the heading is located.

Greeting (Salutation):

Now, point to the mouth because we greet others by saying, "Hello." Point to the greeting on the outline of your friendly letter.

Body:

This section is the main part of our body, so pointing here reminds us that the body is the main part of a letter. Show them the body of a letter then have them point to their bodies.

Closing:

Now grab your pants, shorts, or skirt. While grabbing the material, tell the students that this is "clothing." Clothing sounds like "closing", so grabbing our clothing reminds us of the closing.

Show them the closing of the letter before moving on.

Signature:

Finally, trace an "S" with your foot. The signature is at the foot of the letter, so tracing an "S" with our foot reminds us of the "Signature." Be sure to show them the signature of the letter.

Final Review

To review, I ask for volunteers to race me. We pretend to be Old West gunslingers facing each other across the room with our hands on our hips. Slowly at first then faster and faster, I reach for my head and say "Heading" (or for my foot and say "Signature"). They try to beat me, and it seems the older I get, the closer my students come to beating me.

To determine if they have mastered the parts of the friendly letter, I will point to parts of the letter and ask students to identify them. At this point, my students typically have committed the format of the friendly letter to memory.

Continuing the Lesson

Now that your students have a firm grasp of the basics of the friendly letter, it's time for them to practice writing their own letters. First, have them make a review sheet to use as a reference as they compose their practice letters (see instructions below). Then, give them letter-writing assignments. Finally, test them by having them each write and mail a letter to you at home, at school, or any place you are sure to receive it.

Making the Review Sheet:

In the Appendix, you will find a master for the friendly letter worksheet on the right. Make double-sided copies. Display two samples on the board or a poster and review the five parts of the friendly letter with the students. As you review the parts and their components, students will label them on one side of the worksheet. On the other, they will fill in the blanks with the appropriate information. (See the samples below.) Check for mastery of each part as you review.

The following pages will show you how to explain it to your students.

Heading: I have the students copy the following information:

<table>
<tr><td align="center">Front
(Teacher writes on board.
Students copy on review sheet.)</td><td align="center">Back
(Teacher writes on board.
Students copy on review sheet.)</td></tr>
</table>

| *"Heading"* | *Address*_____
City, State Zip
*Date*_____ | | *12345 Main St.*
Lakewood, CA 90701
January 1, 2000 |

*After the students have copied this information, I take a few minutes to make certain they have memorized the three parts of the heading and its purpose.

I remind them that:

1. The heading can go on the left or the right, but all three lines must align perfectly. I have the students use their pencils to check alignment.

2. Every time I review the parts of a friendly letter, I use "Heading A-C-D" as a mnemonic device to reinforce the parts of the heading. I ask them to touch their heads and say "Heading A-C-D".

    The letters represent:
          A - Address
          C - City, State Zip Code
          D - Date

Greeting (Salutation):
    I remind them that of the purpose of the greeting by saying:

"When you meet your friends at school each day, you don't just start a conversation. You say hello in some way. You begin by **greeting** them. You do the same when you write a letter. Before you begin your message, you should greet the **recipient**, the person to whom you are writing. The greeting is followed by a comma."

    Then I have the students copy the following information:

<table>
<tr><td align="center">Front
(Teacher writes on board.
Students copy on review sheet.)</td><td align="center">Back
(Teacher writes on board.
Students copy on review sheet.)</td></tr>
</table>

| "Heading" | Address_____
City, State Zip
Date_____ | | 12345 Main St._____
Lakewood, CA 90701
January 1, 2000_____ |
| *Greeting,* | | | *Dear Kim,* |

Body:

Front
(Teacher writes on board.
Students copy on review sheet.)

"Heading"	Address
	City, State Zip
	Date
Greeting,	
_____	
_____	
_____ *Body* _____	
_____	

Back
(Teacher writes on board.
Students copy on review sheet.)

```
                    12345 Main St._____
                    Lakewood, CA 90701
                    January 1, 2000_____
Dear Kim,
        What are you learning in school?
We are learning to write letters.
        Give Stinky, your pet snake, a hug
and a kiss for me._____
```

*After the students have copied this information, I take a few minutes to make certain they have memorized the purpose of the body.

I remind them that:
1. The body is the main part of the letter. This is the "conversation" of the letter. You say all the wonderful things you want to say.
2. It can be as short as a sentence or many paragraphs long.

Closing:

Front
(Teacher writes on board.
Students copy on review sheet.)

"Heading"	Address
	City, State Zip
	Date
Greeting,	
_____	
_____	
_____ Body _____	
_____	
_____ *Closing,* _____	

Back
(Teacher writes on board.
Students copy on review sheet.)

```
                    12345 Main St._____
                    Lakewood, CA 90701
                    January 1, 2000_____
Dear Kim,
        What are you learning is school?
We are learning to write letters._____
        Give Stinky, your pet snake, a hug
and  kiss for me._____
_____

            Sincerely,
```

* Remind your students of the greeting story. You don't just start talking without saying hello. Well, you don't just turn around and leave when the conversation is over. You say "goodbye" or "see ya" or something before you go. It's the same for a letter.

A very common closing to a letter is *Sincerely,* but you could also put *Love, Yours Truly, Your Friend,* or anything else that applies, depending on how well you know the person to whom you are writing.

Signature:

Front
(Teacher writes on board.

Back
(Teacher writes on board.

"Heading"	Address City, State Zip Date
Greeting,	
_____	
_____	
_____	
Body	
_____	
Closing,	
Signature	

	12345 Main St. Lakewood, CA 90701 January 1, 2000
Dear Kim,	
_____ What are you learning is school?	
We are learning to write letters.	
_____ Give Stinky, your pet snake, a hug	
and kiss for me.	
_____	
	Sincerely,
	Cyndi Rella

* The signature tells the reader who wrote the letter. It should align with the closing and should always be handwritten. In this way, the reader can be certain that a typed letter was really written by the person who signed it. Anyone can type a name, but signatures can be verified.

Closure:

As students complete the Follow Up assignments, make certain they proof read their letters in order to correct potentially embarrassing mistakes. Also, have them practice adding a P.S. to their letters after the signature. Remember that the P.S. should be short and to the point.

Letter Topics

1. Write a letter to a friend explaining the parts of a letter.
2. Write a letter to a person in the class.
3. Write a letter to your parents telling them about your week.
4. Write a thank you letter to someone for something they've done or given you.
5. Write a letter to someone famous.
6. Write a letter to a former teacher, coach, or instructor. Tell them about your life.

Follow Up Assignments

A. Have students write letters in class. Use the list of Letter Topics for ideas. Monitor their work to make sure they align the heading, greeting, body, closing, and signature.

B. Once your students have mastered letter writing, incorporate the skill into other areas of your curriculum. Here are some ideas:
    1. Find pen pals from other classrooms or home-school groups.
    2. Write letters to characters in literature or history books you are reading.
    3. Write letters to themselves as journal entries.
    4. Give a letter writing test. Have them write a letter to you, and have them mail it to your home, school, or wherever you feel most comfortable receiving it.

The Business Letter

Introduction

      Once the friendly letter is mastered, the business letter is easy to learn. There are six parts to a business letter and a few extra rules to follow. In the Appendix, you will find a master for the business letter worksheet on the right. Make double-sided copies. Display two samples on the board or a poster. Follow the same procedure you did for teaching the friendly letter. Simply add the Inside Address, which includes the name and address of the recipient.

Teaching the Business Letter:

Step A. Review the five parts of a friendly letter using the hand motions. Review the function/purpose of each one. Explain the block style and the addition of the Inside Address. Then, follow the same procedure you did for teaching the friendly letter.

Step B. Label the *heading* on the sample. The students will label it on one side of the worksheet. On the other, they will fill in the blanks with the appropriate information.

    Use: *12345 Main St.*
         Lakewood, CA 90701
         January 1, 2000

```
                          Business Letter
_____                     Step B
_____
_____                     Step C
_____
_____                     Step D
_____:
_____
_____
_____
_____Step E_____
_____
_____
_____
_____,
_____                     Step F
```

Step C. This is the **Inside Address.** It is a necessary part of a business letter and includes the name and address of the recipient. Label the *inside address* on the sample. The students will label it on one side of the worksheet. On the other, they will fill in the blanks with the appropriate information.

    Use: *Mrs. Candy Cane, Elf Coordinator*
         Santa's Workshop
         1001 Arctic Circle
         North Pole, NP 25252

Step D. Point out that the greeting in a business letter, unlike that in a friendly letter, is followed a colon. Label the *greeting*. The students will label it on one side of the worksheet. On the other, they will fill in the blanks with the appropriate information.

    * If the name of the recipient is known - **Dear Mrs. Cane:**
    * If the name of the recipient is unknown - **To Whom It May Concern:**
                                   Or - **Dear Sir or Madam:**

Step E. The body of a business letter should be brief and to the point. Its tone should be formal, but not stiff. Aim for a tone that is friendly, but efficient without the use of slang or poor grammar. Label the *body*. The students will label it on one side of the worksheet. On the other, they will write the following message:

    The students at our school love your peppermint sticks. We would like to order three dozen for our class party. Please send us an order form as soon as possible.

Step F. Although placement depends on the style, the closing and signature follow the same rules as the friendly letter . Label the *closing* and *signature* on the sample. The students will label them on one side of the worksheet. On the other, they will fill in the blanks with the following:

<u>Closing</u>: **Sincerely,**

<u>Signature</u>: *Jack Frost* (Remember that the signature is hand written.)

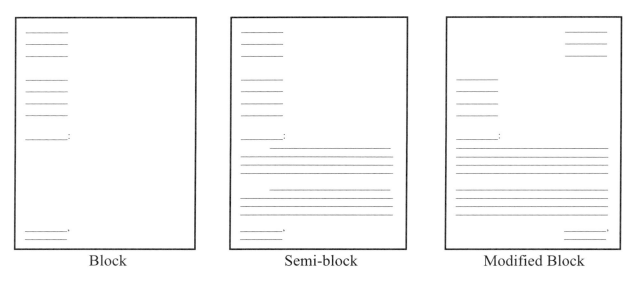

Block	Semi-block	Modified Block

Note: All the lines run along the left margin. There is a space between paragraphs.

Note: All lines run along the left margin, but the paragraphs are indented.

Note: The heading, closure, and signature run along the right margin, and the paragraphs are not indented.

* This would be a good time to explain there are three styles of a business letter. The worksheet example uses the block style. The others are the semi-block and the modified block.

Follow Up Assignments

1. To practice the three styles of business letters, the block, the semi-block, and the modified block, I have my students write a business letter consisting of at least two paragraphs to a toy company.

Paragraph 1 – They are to explain a problem they are having with a toy or game.

Paragraph 2 – They are to explain what they would like the company to do about it.

After editing the letter, they copy it three times — one in each style, block, semi-block format, and modified block format. Finally, they each mount their three letters on a piece of construction paper and label each style. These are great for bulletin boards.

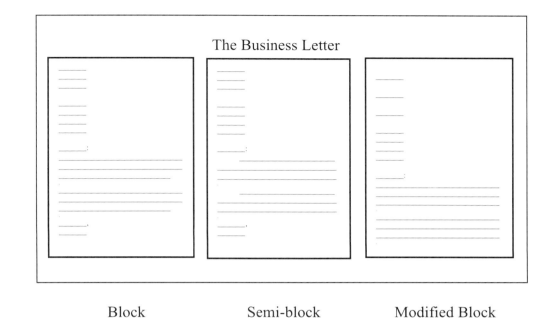

Bulletin
Board
Display

3 Business
Letters
placed on
construction
paper.

The Business Letter

Block   Semi-block   Modified Block

2. Practice writing more business letters by writing letters to politicians about current issues and to companies about their products.

3. Write visitor and convention bureaus in different cities, and request information about local attractions.

4. Conduct a taste test of several different brands of cookies and select a class favorite. Have students write business letters to the winning company describing what they liked most about its cookie. A reply from the company may include coupons for its products. You never know what they might get. What a wonderful reinforcement if the company does reply.

The Research Paper
(A Lesson Plan)

On the following pages, you will find a step by step process for completing a research report and a grading rubric for its evaluation. The Research Report worksheet packet will prove an invaluable aid to your students as they conduct and report on their research. It provides a plan for them to follow and allows them to document completion of each step in a systematic manner.

Elementary school students will write a five-paragraph research paper. The paper will begin with an introductory paragraph. Paragraphs two, three and four will comprise the body of the paper. In the last paragraph students will state their conclusion and may include other interesting facts.

Cover only a few steps at a time, but thoroughly explain the rubric so students understand the importance of doing each step well. Understanding the rubric should help reduce some of the anxiety of undertaking a major project. They can rest assured that successful completion of each step will result in a good grade for the project. Thus, the worksheet will help increase their learning, which is what you want. It will help them get a better grade, which is what they want. Everybody will be happy.

The worksheet is essentially self-explanatory. However, I suggest you pay special attention to the following points as you go through the worksheet.

The **Introductory Paragraph:**

The main purpose of this paragraph is to mentally prepare the students for the project. It helps call to mind what they already know about their topic, and gives them a good starting point from which to proceed. It also helps them formulate theories about their topics and stimulates curiosity about new information they might discover.

Find Information from Three Sources:

The research report is not a book report. The goal of writing a research report is to compile different views, evidence, and facts about a topic in order to produce a document that tells others what the writer has discovered or learned about the topic. Students are to collect this information from several sources. They must then interpret and organize it in order to write a report in their own words. Ultimately, they will share their reports and new-found knowledge with each other and with the teacher. To make sure this

---

Research Report

Follow the steps below to complete your research report.

_____ 1. My topic is: _____

_____ 2. "Introductory Paragraph" - Write a paragraph about your topic. Describe what you already know about your topic and what you would like to know about your topic.

_____ 3. Find information about your topic. You must have at least three sources for your information. Ideas: Books, Magazines, Encyclopedias, Internet, Videos, Other...
Where I found my information:
A. _____
B. _____
C. _____
D. _____

_____ 4. Read through the information on your topic. Write down the important information on your topic. Take notes on:
A. Who are the important people in your topic?
B. What is important about your topic?
C. Where are the important places involved in your topic?
D. When did important events take place?
E. Why are the facts about your topic important?

_____ 5. "I-Search" - Before writing your report, write a paragraph describing your experience researching your topic. Here's how:
Write a paragraph telling me where you found your information, and what information you found to be the most interesting.

---

requirement is met they are to list their sources on the lines under number three on the worksheet. I take off points if they do not have at least three sources.

Take Notes:

It is very important that the students understand that they are to take notes **in their own words**. (This would be a good point to present a mini lesson on paraphrasing.) They are NOT to COPY information word for word from any sources. If they do, they will most likely transfer it directly into their reports. When you return their reports marked "incomplete", they will swear that they did not plagiarize. They will say they wrote the report straight from their notes. It is easier to summarize the information as they research anyway, so train them early not to copy.

Also, over the several days that your students work on this step, be consistent in reminding them to look for THREE MAIN IDEAS to include in their reports. For elementary school students, these will be the main ideas of the three paragraphs in the body of the paper. For middle and high school students, they will become the three sub-topics of their reports.

"I-Search"

There are dozens of different ways to do the I-Search. I like to have the students review their information and its sources, and evaluate what they found. This is a way for them to take a step back from working on the report and absorb what they've learned. While this paragraph may not find its way into the body of the report, writing it provides an opportunity for reflection. They can take pleasure in the fact that they have learned something of interest even if some of the information they found does not apply to the main ideas in their report.

Organize your Information:

This is the pre-writing component of the project. After they have selected their three main ideas, they begin to organize the information into clusters. They might find that they lack sufficient information to fully develop one or more of the main ideas. In this case, they will either have to research some more or select another main idea.

Write Your Report:

Using their pre-writing, the students write their report. This is normally the easy part if they did their research properly. Ask them to double space when they write their final copies. This will leave room for your comments, and for them to make revisions.

Research Report

Follow the steps below to complete your research report.

_____ 1. My topic is: _____

_____ 2. Introductory Paragraph - Write a paragraph about your topic. Describe what you already know about your topic and what you would like to learn about it.

_____ 3. Find information about your topic. <u>You must have at least three different sources for your information.</u> Possible Sources: Books, Magazines, Encyclopedias, Internet, Videos, Other...

Where I found my information:

A. _____

B. _____

C. _____

D. _____

_____ 4. Read through the information on your topic. Write down the important information about your topic. Take notes on:

A. <u>Who</u> are the important people in your topic?

B. <u>What</u> is important about your topic?

C. <u>Where</u> are the important places involved in your topic?

D. <u>When</u> did important events take place?

E. <u>Why</u> are the facts about your topic important?

_____ 5. " I-Search " - Before writing your report, write a paragraph describing your experience researching your topic.

Here's how:

Write a paragraph telling me where you found your information, and what information you found to be the most interesting.

_____ 6. Organize your information:
   A. Read your information and decide:
      "What are the MAIN IDEAS I've discovered?" These
      are your paragraphs.
   B. Write each main idea at the top of a sheet of paper.
      Below each main idea write all the facts related to
      it.

_____ 7. Write your paragraphs (First Draft). Skip lines. Use show-
      not-tell and writing tricks.

_____ 8. Exchange your first draft (include the introductory
      paragraph and "I-Search") with another student and edit
      each other's work. Use the editing process you learned in
      class.

_____ 9. Make any changes needed to improve your report.

_____ 10. Type your final copy on a word processor. Your final
      copy must include three (3) pictures relevant to your
      topic. You may draw the pictures or use photographs.

_____ 11. Prepare your report for grading:
   A. Cover - Your name, title of report, and color
      illustrations your topic.
   B. Attach your pre-writing to the inside cover of your
      report.
   C. Your final copies should be arranged in this order:
      Introductory Paragraph, "I-Search", My Report
      Handouts, the final draft of your report, and a list of the
      resources used.

Research Report
Grading Sheet

Total

_____ Cover (9pts)

      _____ Name + _____ Title of Report + _____ Illustrations

_____ Pre-writing (10 pts)

_____ Introductory Paragraph (10 pts)

      ____ Spelling / Punctuation errors (-2pts)

      ____ Incomplete paragraph (Topic Sentence, supporting sentences, 5-7 sentences, 1 main idea.) (-2pts)

_____ I-Search (10 pts)

      _____ -2 Spelling / Punctuation errors

      _____ -2 Not a complete paragraph (Topic Sent., supporting sentences, 5-7 sent, 1 main idea.)

_____ Each Paragraph of Report (10 pts)

Paragraph #1	Paragraph #2
_____ Quality of information + 5	_____ Quality of information + 5
_____ Quality of paragraph +5	_____ Quality of paragraph +5
_____ Careless mistakes –1	_____ Careless mistakes -1

Paragraph #3

_____ Quality of information + 5

_____ Quality of paragraph +5

_____ Careless mistakes -1

Final Grade

_____ Three pictures (10 pts)

_____ Total Points

Appendix

These two paragraphs can be used for the students to practice their assessments. The first paragraph is an example of a 2 or 3. The second paragraph is an example of a 5 or 6. See Chapter 1.

Paragraph #1

It's important to go to school so we can learn about history, math, reading, writing, and a lot of more things you need to know. School also prepares you for when you need a job. It also teaches you to respect others. It helps you understand life. That's why school is important.

Paragraph #2

For the person wishing to have a productive life, school is an essential prerequisite for achieving that goal. Those who do well in school will get better jobs, be able to think for themselves, and learn the discipline required to do well in life. "I wish I had worked harder when I was in school," are words often spoken by people who failed to take advantage of the opportunities they had while they were young students with fewer responsibilities. So here's a free piece of advice: Do your best in school. You'll be glad you did.

The Accident
by Jane Doe

My friend named Rebecca and I were playing. In our apartments there are hard, rough, red bricks. We were roller blading. My friend got on the bricks. I knew she was going to get hurt. I said get down. She just didn't want to go. I was feeling so solemn.

She laughed like a hyena. She said, "no, I won't get hurt!" I though that she was going to fall on the cement and break some bones. So I got on too so if she was going to fall I would catch her. I was so scared so I fell off. She said, " can jump off too." I went to get her mom because she was on skates.

She said no and jumped off. She laughed at first and them cried. She screamed so loud that you could hear her from Maine. Her mother came and picked her up. She went to the hospital and got a cast. I felt so guilty about it. Everybody blamed it on me.

This story can be used for the students to practice their assessments. See Chapter 1.

The Fall

It was a bright, sunny day in June, 1998. I was at the zoo with my family. In the first few hours I was there I went to the gift shop, bought a hot dog, and smashed a penny. After I did that, we went to look at the lions. I leaned over the rail to get a better look at them.

That was when I felt someone bump into me. I fell in. I tried to move my left arm. I couldn't. It was broken. When I looked up, there was a lion 20 feet away staring right at me. I soiled my pants and y teeth started chattering.

I shouted for help. Someone jumped down to help me and someone else called an ambulance. When they got there, they jumped out of the truck and ran as fast as lightning. They carried me out of the lions den and got me to a helicopter. I started feeling better whin I got to a hospital. When I got out I never leaned over another rail at a zoo.

Writing Assessment Conversion Chart

Directions: After adding the five scores on the writing assessment sheet, use the numbers below to find the writer's final score.

5 = 1	18 = 3.6
6 = 1.2	19 = 3.8
7 = 1.4	20 = 4
8 = 1.6	21 = 4.2
9 = 1.8	22 = 4.4
10 = 2	23 = 4.6
11 = 2.2	24 = 4.8
12 = 2.4	25 = 5
13 = 2.6	26 = 5.2
14 = 2.8	27 = 5.4
15 = 3	28 = 5.6
16 = 3.2	29 = 5.8
17 = 3.4	30 = 6

Writing Prompts

Use these as timed writing assignments or as in-class writing assignments.
(From Chapter 2)

Name: _____

Jobs Prompt
Practical / Informative

Directions: Read "Getting Ready to Write." This section will prepare you for what you are about to write. Next, read "Writing Assignment." Pay close attention because this section tells you what to write.

Getting Ready to Write

Think of the adults in your life and their jobs. Think of your mother, father, grandparents, uncles, and even older sisters and brothers. They all have careers that they've chosen. You will also choose a job in which you will spend many years. What kinds of careers would you fulfilling? What are your interests? Think about the things you like to do and find out if there's a job that allows you to do those things. Some people who like to play video games go on to work with computers. Those who like sports go on to coach or manage sporting events. If you like shopping, there are industries that would pay you to do their purchasing. There are jobs out there to match everyone's interests.

Writing Assignment

First, describe the jobs of your family members. Describe in detail what they do at work. (You may choose to write about only one family member's job.) Second, tell what you would like to do when you grow up. Be sure to explain in detail why you would like this job. Finally, describe the things you will have to do to get this job. Will it require specialized training or education after high-school? Would it help to know people in the field?

Name: _____

My Holiday Wish for the World
Analytical / Expository

Directions: Read "Getting Ready to Write." This section will prepare you for what you are about to write. Next, read "Writing Assignment." Pay close attention because this section tells you what to write.

Getting Ready to Write

December is a time for special holidays for many people in the world. Christmas, Hanukkah, New Year's Eve, and Kwanza are all holidays that cause people to pause and reflect upon the things that are important to them. When we think of how much we have it is only natural to think about the people who are less fortunate than ourselves. Many people cannot enjoy this season because of serious problems in their lives. This writing assignment is going to ask you consider a challenge someone may face. It may be crime, drugs, poverty, pollution, loneliness, discrimination, or abuse. Think of people who are struggling in life who could use a helping hand.

Writing Assignment

If you were given a holiday wish for the world, what would it be? Begin your essay by describing a major problem in the world. Explain in detail how this problem is affecting people. Next, describe your wish for the world. Explain why the world would be a better place if your wish were granted. Finally, explain the things you might do to help make this wish come true.

Literature Character Like Me
(Sensory / Descriptive) (Practical / Informative)

Directions: Read "Getting Ready to Write." This section will prepare you for what you are about to write. Next, read "Writing Assignment." Pay close attention because this section tells you what to write.

Getting Ready to Write

One of the great things about reading a book is that you get to know some of its characters so well. Some characters, such as the hero, you love and others, such as the villain, you hate. What makes reading a book a truly great experience is meeting a character who reminds us of ourselves. You are going to write about a character who either reminds you of yourself or whose traits you would like to emulate. Think about the books you have enjoyed the most, and think about the characters you found the most interesting.

Writing Assignment

Select a literature character who reminds you of yourself. This character might have qualities similar to your own or may possess some you would like to emulate.

Begin by describing the character and identifying the book in which he or she appears. Be sure to explain what you find interesting about the character. Next, compare this character to yourself. What was it about this character that impressed you? What traits do you and this character share? Use many details, and be as specific as possible.

Name: _____

Dreams
Imaginative / Narrative

Directions: Read "Getting Ready to Write." This section will prepare you for what you are about to write. Next, read "Writing Assignment." Pay close attention because this section tells you what to write.

Getting Ready to Write

Everybody dreams. Sometimes we wake up in the morning with an exciting dream still fresh in our minds. Sometimes our mind starts to wander, and before we know it, we've spent the last several minutes daydreaming.

What do you dream about? Do you dream of being the gold medal winner in Olympic figure skating? Do you dream of being the hero by saving your friends from a terrible disaster? Or do you dream about sharing an adventure with a special person? This will be your chance to write about an exciting dream.

Writing Assignment

Write about a dream or daydream that was very exciting. Write about the dream as if it were a story. This means that it should have all the elements of a story including a beginning, a middle, and an end. Include as many show-not-tell: setting and emotions as possible. Try to make your readers feel as though they are experiencing the action in the dream with you. Have fun!

Letter to the Editor

Persuasive - Analytical / Expository

Directions: Read "Getting Ready to Write." This section will prepare you for what you are about to write. Next, read "Writing Assignment." Pay close attention because this section tells you what to write.

Getting Ready to Write

Open up most newspapers and you will find an opinion page or letters to the editor. In these sections, people give their opinions about situations they think should be changed, and they try to persuade the readers of the paper to agree with their point of view. You are going to write such a letter and try to convince readers to agree with your opinion about a topic that is very important to you. Begin by thinking of a situation in your school, neighborhood, city, country, or even the world that you would like to change.

Writing Assignment

Opinions are like belly-buttons; everybody has one. Consider issues that are important to you. Select a problem you would like to see resolved or an attitude you would like to change. Then, compose a letter to the editor of a local paper describing the present situation and its importance. Next, describe the consequences of allowing the situation to persist. Finally, describe your solution to the problem or your point of view regarding the attitude with which you are in disagreement. Explain specific steps people should take to effect the change you suggest.

Name: _____

Family Story
Imaginative / Narrative

Directions: Read "Getting Ready to Write." This section will prepare you for what you are about to write. Next, read "Writing Assignment." Pay close attention because this section tells you what to write.

Getting Ready to Write

"Remember the time that ..." It seems that every family has a collection of stories to tell whenever the whole family gets together. "Remember the time Grandma thought it was Sunday and got all dressed up for church, only to find out it was Saturday. She walked right into the ..." Grandma will never live that one down. There probably are stories all of us would just as soon forget, but our beloved relatives just love to tell those stories every time the family gathers. For this assignment, you are going to write about one of those family stories. You can write about one which involved you, or choose a story that you've heard so many times, you feel like you were there when it occurred.

Writing Assignment

Write about a story that is told by your family over and over again. Begin the story by describing the person who usually tells it. Mom? Dad? Uncle Bob? Describe the setting where the story is usually told. Around the Christmas tree? At a campsite? Then write the story and make us feel as if we are there, listening to the story with you. Make sure the story has a beginning, a middle, and an end.

Prepositions

about	concerning	since
above	down	through
across	during	throughout
after	except	to
against	for	toward
along	from	under
amid	in	underneath
among	inside	until
around	into	up
at	like	upon
atop	near	with
before	of	within
behind	off	without
below	on	
beneath	onto	
beside	out	
between	outside	
beyond	over	
but (meaning except)	past	
by	regarding	

The following pages are the inserts for your students' writing folders. They are the cover pages for each section of the folder. They tell the students what work belongs in each section. Photocopy each page for every student.

(From Chapter 7)

The following items belong in this section:

1. Writing Assessment Checklist

2. Writing Assessment Chart

3. Writing Assessment Sheets

4. _____

5. _____

Show -not- Tell

The following items belong in this section:

    1. All show-not-tell clusters (pre-writing) we make in class or for homework.

        A. Setting   B. Emotions   C. Others

    2. All final drafts of show-not-tell paragraphs.

    3. Lists of show-not-tell words.

        A. Sound, Sight, Touch, Smell, and Taste Words

        B. "Said" words.

        D. Dead Words.

    4. _____

    5. _____

The following items belong in this section:

1. Vocabulary words I like. After each vocabulary lesson, make a list of two or three words from that lesson which you would like to use in your writing.

2. Put all picture dictionary worksheets together.

3. Put all Let Me Count the Ways worksheets together.

4. _____

5. _____

After each vocabulary lesson, make a list of two or three words from that lesson which you would like to use in your writing.

_____   _____   _____   _____

_____   _____   _____   _____

_____   _____   _____   _____

_____   _____   _____   _____

_____   _____   _____   _____

_____   _____   _____   _____

_____   _____   _____   _____

_____   _____   _____   _____

_____   _____   _____   _____

_____   _____   _____   _____

_____   _____   _____   _____

The following items belong in this section:

    1. ALL of the worksheets that we do in class to learn writing tricks.

    2. Keep a list of writing tricks that we've learned here:

A. _____   B. _____

C. _____   D. _____

E. _____   F. _____

G. _____   H. _____

I. _____   J. _____

K. _____   L. _____

M. _____   N. _____

O. _____   P. _____

My writing goal is:

_____

What I am doing well:

_____
_____
_____
_____
_____

What I need to work on:

_____
_____
_____
_____
_____

Elements
of a Story

Teacher Copy - Transparency

Introduction – The beginning of the story where the
characters and setting are introduced.

Conflict – The problem of the story that needs to be solved.

Rising Action – The major events in a story that lead from
the problem to the solution.

Climax – The major turning point of the story where the
conflict's resolution is uncertain.

Resolution – How the problem is solved.

Epilogue – The part where the story comes to an end and loose
ends are tied up.

Elements of a Story

Introduction - _____

_____

_____

Conflict - _____

_____

Rising Action - _____

_____

_____

Climax - _____

_____

Resolution - _____

_____

Epilogue - _____

_____

Letter Outlines

Friendly Letter and Business Letter
(From Chapter 8)

Friendly Letter

_____

_____

_____

_____,

_____

_____

_____

_____

_____

_____,

_____

Business Letter

_____

_____

_____

_____

_____

_____

_____

_____:

_____

_____

_____

_____

_____

_____

_____,

_____